United States
Department of
Agriculture

Forest Service

Southern
Research Station

Research Paper
SRS–47

Diameter Growth of Subtropical Trees in Puerto Rico

Thomas J. Brandeis

Author:

Thomas J. Brandeis, Research Forester, U.S. Forest Service, Southern
Research Station, Forest Inventory and Analysis, Knoxville, TN 37919.

Cover photo: Plantation of mahoe (*Hibiscus elatus* Sw.) in the Cambalache Commonwealth Forest,
Arecibo, Puerto Rico.

DISCLAIMER

The use of trade or firm names in this publication is for reader information and does not imply
endorsement by the U.S. Department of Agriculture of any product or service.

November 2009

Southern Research Station
200 W.T. Weaver Blvd.
Asheville, NC 28804

Diameter Growth of Subtropical Trees in Puerto Rico

Thomas J. Brandeis

Abstract

Puerto Rico's forests consist of young, secondary stands still recovering from a long history of island-wide deforestation that largely abated in the mid-20th century. Limited knowledge about growth rates of subtropical tree species in these forests makes it difficult to accurately predict forest yield, biomass accumulation, and carbon sequestration. This study presents mean annual increases (periodic annual increment) in tree diameter at breast height among trees measured by the forest inventories of Puerto Rico; this information is given for each forested life zone, by species, then by species and crown class, and by crown position class. Additionally, the study presents mean periodic annual increment values calculated for commercial species by tree class (growing stock and cull). From 1980 to 2008, mean diameter at breast height periodic annual increment was 0.35 cm/year for 4,026 trees remeasured by the forest inventory; growth rate averaged 0.20 cm/year in subtropical dry forests, 0.37 cm/year in subtropical moist forests, 0.36 cm/year in subtropical wet/rain forests, and 0.20 cm/year in lower montane forests.

Keywords: Caribbean, crown position, FIA, periodic annual increment, secondary forest.

Introduction

Puerto Rico's forests consist of young, secondary stands still recovering (Birdsey and Weaver 1982, Brandeis and others 2007, Franco and others 1997) from a long history of island-wide deforestation that largely abated in the mid-20th century (Grau and others 2003, Rudel and others 2000, Wadsworth 1950). Such secondary forest ecosystems cover an increasing percentage of the tropical and subtropical landscape not only in the Caribbean but also globally (Brown and Lugo 1990, Finegan 1996, Myster 2004). We need to better understand secondary forest development and function if resource management and land use planning is to be informed and effective.

Knowledge of tree growth rates is fundamental to understanding forest function, and can support estimates of biomass accumulation, carbon sequestration, and commodity production potential. Previous studies on long-term research plots have focused on growth rates of many tree species in the subtropical wet, subtropical rain, lower montane wet, and lower montane rain forest life zones of the Luquillo Mountains of Puerto Rico (Crow and Weaver 1977, Schmidt and Weaver 1981, Weaver 1979, Weaver and Birdsey 1990). [See Ewel and Whitmore (1973) for descriptions of these Holdridge life zones.] Studies also have focused—albeit less intensively—on growth rates of species in the lower ecological zones and in forests at earlier successional stages, including estimated growth rates in the subtropical dry forest (Briscoe 1962) and the subtropical moist forest (Weaver 1979, Weaver and Nieves 1978). Weaver and Birdsey (1990) were the first to use forest inventory remeasurements (from 1980 to 1985) to estimate growth rates for trees across the entire island, but that inventory excluded some forest types, particularly in the subtropical dry forest life zone, that were not considered to have the potential for commercial wood products production (Birdsey and Weaver 1982) and therefore might not be representative of the full range of growth rates.

The latest forest inventory results greatly increased the number of remeasured trees and can provide estimates of tree growth over a wider range of environmental conditions for more species. The increased sampling allows growth rate estimation not only for more species but also for species under different levels of competition as reflected by the tree's relative position in the canopy. For *Bucida buceras* L. trees in subtropical dry forests, relative canopy position has been found a useful benchmark of growth potential.

The objectives of this study were to calculate growth among trees measured by the forest inventories of Puerto Rico, with growth represented by annual increases (periodic annual increment, or PAI) in tree diameter at breast height (d.b.h.). Mean PAI values were calculated for each forested life zone, by species, then by species and crown position, and by crown class. Additionally, mean PAI values were calculated for commercial species by tree class (growing stock and cull).

Methods

Study Area

The data for this study were collected on the main island of the Commonwealth of Puerto Rico, centered on 18°15' N. by 66°30' W. Birdsey and Weaver (1982) and Ewel and Whitmore (1973) give excellent descriptions of the Holdridge life zones commonly used to describe these subtropical forests and the species found in them. Tree species nomenclature used here comes from the U.S. Department of Agriculture, Natural Resources Conservation Service, Plants Database (U.S. Department of Agriculture, Natural Resources Conservation Service 2006).

Forest Inventories and Tree Measurements

The tree measurements came from four forest inventories of Puerto Rico conducted by the Forest Service, Forest Inventory and Analysis (FIA) Program. These inventories took place in 1980, 1990, 2001–04, and 2006–09. For details on these inventories, see Birdsey and Weaver (1982), Franco and others (1997), and Brandeis and others (2007). The first two forest inventories (1980 and 1990) were each completed in 1 year. More recent inventories spread measurements over 4 years, with each forest inventory plot remeasured every 5 years. Forest inventory plots are permanent, and each tree in the plot is mapped and remeasured with each revisit to the plot. Only a small percentage of the trees have been measured since 1980, however, due to changes in the forest inventory design between 1990 and 2001, as well as damage and mortality on some plots associated with the passages of Hurricanes Hugo (1989) and Georges (1998). Therefore, while a small number of trees has been measured four times for more than 20 years, most of the data used to calculate PAI comes from two remeasurements separated by 5 or 10 years.

Tree diameters were measured at a height of 1.4 m (*sensu* U.S. Department of Agriculture Forest Service 2002) for stems with d.b.h. ≥ 2.5 cm. Trees with abnormal forms and those with estimated diameters were removed from the dataset. While bole shrinkage can naturally occur, 250 trees with negative growth (decreases in d.b.h. in subsequent remeasurements) were excluded from this study's dataset. The exclusion of these data might skew results toward greater average growth rates.

Tree Crown Rating

Field crews classified each tree crown class in relation to the sunlight received and proximity to neighboring trees, using these categories: open grown, dominant, codominant, intermediate, and suppressed (or overtopped). The crown classifications were based on definitions in the forest inventory field manual of the U.S. Department of Agriculture Forest Service (2002). Open-grown trees have crowns that receive full sunlight from above and all sides throughout most of their life. Dominant trees have crowns that rise above the general level of the crown cover and get full sunlight from above and partly from the sides; these trees are taller than the average trees in the stand and their crowns are well developed, but they could be somewhat crowded by other trees on the sides. Codominant trees have medium-sized crowns growing at the general level of the crown canopy and receiving full overhead light, but surrounding trees restrict some sunlight from the sides. In stagnated stands, codominant trees have small crowns and are crowded on the sides. Intermediate trees are shorter than dominants and codominants, but their crowns extend into the canopy of codominant and dominant trees and get little direct sunlight from above and none from the sides. As a result, intermediates usually have small crowns and are very crowded from the sides. Suppressed, or overtopped, trees have crowns entirely below the general level of the crown canopy and receive no sunlight from above or the sides.

To simplify analysis and increase the number of sample trees in each category, two broader categories of relative crown position also were created: overstory and understory. The overstory crown position consists of open-grown, dominant, and codominant trees. The understory crown position consists of intermediate and suppressed trees.

Tree Class Rating

To measure trees of commercial species, growing-stock classifications also were used. The definition of growing stock is a live tree of a commercial species that possesses (or has the potential to produce, in the case of poletimber-sized trees) at least one-third of the gross board-foot volume in sound wood. The logs must meet merchantable grade, soundness, and size requirements. Trees that do not meet growing-stock specifications are called "cull." No distinctions were made in this study between rough and rotten cull.

Results

A total of 4,026 trees were measured at least twice for growth estimates, and their overall mean d.b.h. PAI was 0.35 cm/year (table 1). Number of trees measured, mean d.b.h. PAI, standard error of the mean, standard deviation of the mean, and maximum observed PAI for each life zone are presented in table 1. These same statistics are presented by species and crown class in appendix table A.1, by species and crown position in appendix table A.2, and by commercial species and tree class in appendix table A.3.

Individual trees of several species exhibited growth rates over 2.5 cm/year in this study. They were *Eucalyptus robusta* Sm. (5.84 cm/year), *Pithecellobium unguis-cati* (L.) Benth. (5.74 cm/year), *Cordia sulcata* DC. (5.08 cm/year), *Cecropia schreberiana* Miq. (4.30 cm/year), *Roystonea borinquena* O.F. Cook (4.00 cm/year), *Spathodea campanulata* P. Beauv. (3.76 cm/year), *Inga laurina* (Sw.) Willd. (3.32 cm/year), *Ficus citrifolia* Mill. (3.05 cm/year), *Dendropanax arboreus* (L.) Decne. & Planch. ex Britton (3.03 cm/year), *Pouteria multiflora* (A. DC.) Eyma (3.00 cm/year), *Guarea guidonia* (L.) Sleumer (2.90 cm/year), *Inga vera* Willd. (2.88 cm/year), *Pithecellobium dulce* (Roxb.) Benth. (2.74 cm/year), *Zanthoxylum martinicense* (Lam.) DC. (2.62 cm/year), *Erythrina poeppigiana* (Walp.) O.F. Cook (2.61 cm/year) and *Inga vera* Willd. (2.54 cm/year).

Table 1—Diameter at breast height (1.4 m) periodic annual increments (PAI) by Holdridge life zone with number of trees measured, standard error of the mean, standard deviation of the mean, and maximum observed PAI increase from Puerto Rico forest inventory data

Life zone	N	Periodic annual increments			
		Mean	SE	SD	Max
Subtropical dry	307	0.20	0.03	0.45	5.74
Subtropical moist	2,315	0.37	0.01	0.48	4.30
Subtropical wet/rain	1,292	0.36	0.01	0.51	5.84
Lower montane	112	0.20	0.02	0.24	1.28
All life zones	4,026	0.35	0.01	0.49	5.84

N = number of trees measured; SE = standard error of the mean; SD = standard deviation of the mean; Max = maximum observed.

Conclusions

The mean d.b.h. PAI of 0.35 cm/year for trees remeasured by the forest inventory from 1980 to 2008 averages growth rates over a broad range of environmental conditions and species. While it was higher than the mean of 0.21 cm/year previously reported for the island by Weaver and Birdsey (1990) in their analysis of a partial remeasurement of the forest inventory plots in 1985, subsequent growth measurements in long-term research plots at several sites across the island have shown values that range from 0.13 to 0.47 cm/year (table 2). For growth rates in specific life zones, 0.20 cm/year in subtropical dry forests generally agrees with values observed by Briscoe (1962) for naturally and artificially regenerated stands on limestone substrate. Subtropical moist forests consistently show the highest potential mean growth rates on the island, followed by subtropical wet forests (Weaver 1979). Growth rates decrease moving from subtropical wet forest into the lower montane forest, as shown in previous studies. Weaver (1983) showed lower growth rates in the lower montane forests (0.10 to 0.03 cm/year, depending on the forest type) when compared to the adjacent subtropical wet forests (0.15 to 0.23 cm/year, depending on forest type), and theorized that increased cloud cover and poorly drained soils found at higher elevations in Puerto Rico limit productivity.

The tree growth estimates of Weaver and Birdsey (1990) might be lower than current estimates. The later, expanded inventory surveyed more understocked and early successional stands where trees were colonizing abandoned agricultural land and had less competition for site resources. A greater percentage of trees with higher growth rates can be expected in the later sampling. Silvicultural research in Puerto Rico has shown that some species' growth rates respond positively to competition reduction from stand thinning. For example, overstory (codominant) tabonuco (*Dacryodes excelsa* Vahl) trees in thinned stands had growth rates of 0.70 cm/year, while growth in undisturbed plots ranged from 0.15 to 0.23 cm/year (Weaver 1983).

Disturbance by hurricanes can have an effect on survivor growth rates similar to thinning. Two major hurricanes, Hurricane Hugo in 1989 and Hurricane Georges in 1998, hit Puerto Rican forest stands during the remeasurement period. Authors of growth studies done before the passage of Hurricane Hugo in 1989 speculated that a large percentage of the trees were suppressed and in "steady state" since last released by disturbance caused by Hurricane Ciprián in 1932 (Crow and Weaver 1977; Weaver 1979, 1983).

Table 2—Observed subtropical tree growth rates in Puerto Rico by location, Holdridge life zone and forest-type association, time period of the measurements, diameter periodic annual increments, relevant notes on the study, and the bibliographic source

Location	Holdridge life zone and forest-type association	Time period	PAI		Notes	Source
		year	*cm/year*			
Guánica	Dry	17	0.13	0.36	Natural and artificial regeneration on karst substrate	Briscoe 1962
Luquillo Mtns.	Lower montane (elfin, palm, palo colorado, tabonuco)	18	0.30	0.60	Unthinned stands, with some prior tree removals	Crow and Weaver 1977
Rio Piedras	Moist	32	0.22		Thinned stands	Weaver and Nieves 1978
Luquillo Mtns.	Wet, rain, and lower montane	5	0.03	0.36	Thinned and unmanaged stands	Weaver 1983
San Juan, St. Just	Moist	2	0.47		Thinned, early secondary stands	Weaver 1979
Piñones	Moist (mangrove)	37	0.46		Natural regeneration after clearing	Weaver 1979
Toro Negro	Lower montane wet (palo colorado)	24	0.15		Thinned stands	Weaver 1979
Maricao	Lower montane wet	24	0.12		Thinned stands on serpentine substrate	Weaver 1979
Luquillo Mtns.	Moist (palo colorado)	27	0.25		Thinned stands	Schmidt and Weaver 1981
Islandwide	All life zones	5	0.21		Partial survey in 1985, with some forest types excluded	Weaver and Birdsey 1990

PAI = periodic annual increments.

Hurricane-force winds more heavily damage crowns of larger trees, create gaps for forest regeneration, and reduce stand basal area (Pascarella and others 2004, Weaver 1989, Zimmerman and others 1994). Weaver (1983) states that "the critical element determining whether increment was slow or rapid would be the amount of time between major storms."

Maximum observed growth rates were much higher than those reported in previous studies. Growth rates exceeding 5 cm/year were found, while previous studies only found maximum rates of 1 to 2 cm/year, although growth rates exceeding 2.5 cm/year have been observed in Puerto Rico's subtropical wet forests [Wadsworth (1958) as cited in Wadsworth (1997)]. However, these maximum growth rates were observed in individual trees over short periods of time (during a 5- to 10-year period between remeasurements) and most likely represent trees growing under ideal environmental conditions with little to no competition. These extreme growth rates are not fully representative of the species' average growth; rather they express potential for growth under excellent growing conditions. This study's larger sample size and wider variety of surveyed sites— particularly open, recently reverted forests where trees are still free from neighboring competition—increase the probability of sampling trees that grow under such favorable environments.

The results of this study produce a more comprehensive assessment of the average and potential growth, biomass accumulation, and carbon sequestration of Caribbean subtropical forest trees. This study helps address the need for information on tree growth among a wide variety of species and growing conditions, and such information can validate existing growth and yield models as well as create new ones. With such models, we gain the capacity to project secondary stand development into the future and choose management options that move these forests toward the structural and compositional conditions that deliver much needed forest ecosystem services to island inhabitants.

Acknowledgments

I would like to thank Ariel Lugo and Eileen Helmer of the Forest Service's International Institute of Tropical Forestry; Esther Rojas of the Puerto Rican Conservation Foundation; and Jonathan Buford, Johanna D'Arcy, Orlando Díaz, Christopher Furr, Jeremy Grayson, Humfredo Marcano, Omar Monsegur, Luis Ortíz, Humberto Rodriguez, Jim Schiller, and Iván Vicéns for field data collection. I would also like to thank Dr. Peter Weaver and Dr. Christopher Oswalt for their comments and suggestions on the draft manuscript.

Literature Cited

Birdsey, R.A.; Weaver, P.L. 1982. The forest resources of Puerto Rico. Resour. Bull. SO–85. New Orleans: U.S. Department of Agriculture Forest Service, Southern Forest Experiment Station. 56 p.

Brandeis, T.J.; Helmer, E.H.; Oswalt, S.N. 2007. The status of Puerto Rico's forests, 2003. Resour. Bull. SRS–119. Asheville, NC: U.S. Department of Agriculture Forest Service, Southern Research Station. 75 p.

Briscoe, C.B. 1962. Tree diameter growth in the dry limestone hills. Trop. For. Notes 12. Río Piedras, PR: U.S. Department of Agriculture Forest Service, Tropical Forest Research Center. 2 p.

Brown, S.; Lugo, A.E. 1990. Tropical secondary forests. Journal of Tropical Ecology. 6: 1–32.

Crow, T.R.; Weaver, P.L. 1977. Tree growth in moist tropical forest of Puerto Rico. Res. Pap. ITF–22. Río Piedras, PR: U.S. Department of Agriculture Forest Service, Institute of Tropical Forestry. 17 p.

Ewel, J.J.; Whitmore, J.L. 1973. The ecological life zones of Puerto Rico and the US Virgin Islands. Res. Pap. ITF–18. Río Piedras, PR: U.S. Department of Agriculture Forest Service, Institute of Tropical Forestry. 72 p.

Finegan, B. 1996. Pattern and process in neotropical secondary rain forests: the first 100 years of succession. Tree. 11: 119–124.

Franco, P.A.; Weaver, P.L.; Eggen-McIntosh, S. 1997. Forest resources of Puerto Rico, 1990. Resour. Bull. SRS–22. Asheville, NC: U.S. Department of Agriculture Forest Service, Southern Research Station. 45 p.

Grau, R.H.; Aide, T.M.; Zimmerman, J.K. [and others]. 2003. The ecological consequences of socioeconomic and land-use changes in postagriculture Puerto Rico. BioScience. 53: 1159–1168.

Myster, R.W. 2004. Post-agricultural invasion, establishment, and growth of neotropical trees. The Botanical Review. 70: 381–402.

Pascarella, J.B.; Aide, T.M.; Zimmerman, J.K. 2004. Short-term response of secondary forests to hurricane disturbance in Puerto Rico, USA. Forest Ecology and Management. 199: 379–393.

Rudel, T.K.; Pérez-Lugo, M.; Zichal, H. 2000. When fields revert to forest: development and spontaneous reforestation in post-war Puerto Rico. The Professional Geographer. 52: 386–397.

Schmidt, R.; Weaver, P.L. 1981. Tree diameter increment in the subtropical moist life zone of Puerto Rico. Turrialba. 31: 261–263.

U.S. Department of Agriculture Forest Service. 2002. Field procedures for Puerto Rico and the Virgin Islands. Suppl. C to SRS Reg. Man. 1.56. http://srsfia2.fs.fed.us/data_acquisition/manual.shtml. [Date accessed: June, 2006].

Wadsworth, F.H. 1950. Notes on the climax forests of Puerto Rico and their destruction and conservation prior to 1900. Caribbean Forester. 11: 38–47.

Wadsworth, F.H. 1958. Tropical rain forest. In: Proceedings of the 4th World Forestry Congress. Dehra Dun, India: Government of India, Manager of Publications: 119–129.

Wadsworth, F.H. 1997. Forest production for tropical America. Agric. Handb. 710. Washington, DC: U.S. Department of Agriculture. 563 p.

Weaver, P.L. 1979. Tree growth in several tropical forests of Puerto Rico. Res. Pap. SO–152. New Orleans: U.S. Department of Agriculture Forest Service, Southern Forest Experiment Station. 15 p.

Weaver, P.L. 1983. Tree growth and stand changes in the subtropical life zones of the Luquillo Mountains of Puerto Rico. Res. Pap. SO–190. New Orleans: U.S. Department of Agriculture Forest Service, Southern Forest Experiment Station. 24 p.

Weaver, P.L. 1989. Forest changes after hurricanes in Puerto Rico's Luquillo Mountains. Interciencia. 14: 181–192.

Weaver, P.L.; Birdsey, R.A. 1990. Growth of secondary forest in Puerto Rico between 1980 and 1985. Turrialba. 40: 12–22.

Weaver, P.L.; Nieves, L.O. 1978. Periodic annual dbh increment in a subtropical moist forest dominated by Syzygium jambos (L) Alston. Turrialba. 28: 253–256.

Zimmerman, J.K.; Everham, E.M., III; Waide, R.B. [and others]. 1994. Responses of tree species to hurricane winds in subtropical wet forest in Puerto Rico: implications for tropical tree life histories. Journal of Ecology. 82: 911–922.

Appendix

Table A.1—Diameter at breast height (1.4 m) periodic annual increments (PAI, cm) by species and crown class with number of trees measured, standard error of the mean, standard deviation of the mean, and maximum observed PAI increase from Puerto Rico forest inventory data

Species[1]	Crown class	N	Mean	SE	SD	Max
			\multicolumn{4}{c}{Periodic annual increments}			
Acacia farnesiana (L.) Willd.	Codominant	5	0.50	0.15	0.34	0.86
Acrocomia media O.F. Cook	Codominant	1	0.04			0.04
Adelia ricinella L.	Intermediate	1	0.02			0.02
Adenanthera pavonina L.	Codominant	7	1.15	0.16	0.42	1.86
	Intermediate	1	1.48			1.48
	Overtopped	15	0.25	0.09	0.36	1.28
Albizia procera (Roxb.) Benth.	Dominant	13	0.67	0.18	0.64	2.16
	Codominant	14	0.74	0.17	0.64	2.22
	Intermediate	1	0.04			0.04
	Overtopped	2	0.14	0.02	0.03	0.16
Alchornea latifolia Sw.	Open grown	1	0.28			0.28
	Dominant	3	0.19	0.13	0.22	0.44
	Codominant	10	0.32	0.09	0.29	1.04
	Intermediate	7	0.17	0.04	0.10	0.32
	Overtopped	2	0.33	0.13	0.18	0.46
	Overtopped	1	0.00			0.00
Amyris elemifera L.	Codominant	8	0.14	0.04	0.13	0.42
	Intermediate	4	0.05	0.02	0.05	0.10
	Overtopped	8	0.04	0.01	0.04	0.08
Andira inermis (W. Wright) Kunth ex DC.	Open grown	1	1.05			1.05
	Dominant	16	0.33	0.08	0.34	1.26
	Codominant	72	0.22	0.03	0.23	0.96
	Intermediate	32	0.16	0.04	0.22	0.80
	Overtopped	12	0.09	0.03	0.10	0.22
Annona muricata L.	Codominant	2	0.25	0.23	0.33	0.48
	Intermediate	2	0.36	0.24	0.34	0.60
	Codominant	2	0.09	0.09	0.13	0.18
A. squamosa L.	Dominant	1	0.00			0.00
	Codominant	1	0.92			0.92
Antirhea obtusifolia Urb.	Intermediate	1	0.16			0.16
	Codominant	11	0.09	0.03	0.09	0.28
	Intermediate	3	0.08	0.03	0.05	0.14
	Overtopped	8	0.06	0.03	0.08	0.24
Artocarpus altilis (Parkinson) Fosberg	Dominant	6	0.38	0.15	0.37	0.87
	Codominant	13	0.22	0.04	0.15	0.58
	Intermediate	5	0.17	0.08	0.18	0.44
	Overtopped	1	0.01			0.01
Avicennia germinans (L.) L.	Dominant	4	0.04	0.04	0.07	0.14
	Codominant	10	0.30	0.14	0.46	1.20

continued

Table A.1—Diameter at breast height (1.4 m) periodic annual increments (PAI, cm) by species and crown class with number of trees measured, standard error of the mean, standard deviation of the mean, and maximum observed PAI increase from Puerto Rico forest inventory data (continued)

Species[a]	Crown class	N	Periodic annual increments			
			Mean	SE	SD	Max
Avicennia germinans (L.) L. (continued)	Overtopped	1	0.10			0.10
Banara portoricensis Krug & Urb.	Intermediate	1	0.32			0.32
	Dominant	1	0.34			0.34
Bourreria succulenta Jacq.	Dominant	1	0.08			0.08
	Codominant	27	0.15	0.05	0.24	0.98
	Intermediate	6	0.10	0.06	0.14	0.32
	Intermediate	2	0.10	0.02	0.03	0.12
Buchenavia tetraphylla (Aubl.) Howard	Dominant	5	0.79	0.20	0.44	1.45
	Codominant	1	0.30			0.30
	Overtopped	1	0.04			0.04
Bucida buceras L.	Open grown	2	0.48	0.06	0.08	0.54
	Dominant	4	0.31	0.05	0.10	0.42
	Codominant	6	0.28	0.09	0.22	0.60
	Intermediate	1	0.00			0.00
	Open grown	2	0.56	0.32	0.45	0.88
	Dominant	14	0.49	0.18	0.68	2.48
	Codominant	46	0.31	0.04	0.27	1.06
	Intermediate	1	0.05			0.05
	Overtopped	3	0.07	0.04	0.06	0.12
Byrsonima lucida (Mill.) DC.	Dominant	1	0.06			0.06
	Codominant	5	0.11	0.03	0.07	0.22
B. spicata (Cav.) Kunth	Dominant	4	0.45	0.03	0.06	0.52
	Codominant	7	0.51	0.20	0.53	1.56
	Intermediate	2	0.36	0.16	0.23	0.52
B. wadsworthii Little	Intermediate	1	0.02			0.02
	Dominant	10	0.49	0.05	0.16	0.80
	Codominant	12	0.47	0.13	0.44	1.38
	Intermediate	2	0.40	0.37	0.52	0.76
	Overtopped	8	0.28	0.09	0.25	0.80
Canella winterana (L.) Gaertn.	Codominant	3	0.13	0.02	0.03	0.16
	Overtopped	1	0.16			0.16
Capparis baducca L.	Intermediate	1	0.04			0.04
	Overtopped	1	0.00			0.00
	Codominant	1	0.08			0.08
C. flexuosa (L.) L.	Intermediate	2	0.02	0.02	0.03	0.04
	Codominant	4	0.05	0.04	0.08	0.16
	Intermediate	2	0.03	0.01	0.01	0.04
	Codominant	1	0.10			0.10
Casearia arborea (Rich.) Urb.	Codominant	5	0.25	0.09	0.20	0.48
	Intermediate	11	0.20	0.04	0.13	0.42
	Overtopped	6	0.11	0.08	0.18	0.48

continued

Table A.1—Diameter at breast height (1.4 m) periodic annual increments (PAI, cm) by species and crown class with number of trees measured, standard error of the mean, standard deviation of the mean, and maximum observed PAI increase from Puerto Rico forest inventory data (continued)

| Species[a] | Crown class | N | Periodic annual increments | | | |
			Mean	SE	SD	Max
Casearia decandra Jacq.	Intermediate	6	0.03	0.02	0.04	0.10
	Overtopped	7	0.02	0.01	0.02	0.05
C. guianensis (Aubl.) Urb.	Dominant	1	0.06	—	—	0.06
	Codominant	7	0.18	0.06	0.15	0.42
	Intermediate	14	0.17	0.04	0.13	0.36
	Overtopped	50	0.08	0.01	0.10	0.50
	Codominant	5	0.19	0.09	0.19	0.52
	Intermediate	19	0.11	0.03	0.15	0.48
	Overtopped	23	0.09	0.02	0.10	0.36
Cassine xylocarpa Vent.	Codominant	5	0.03	0.02	0.04	0.10
Castilla elastica Sessé	Codominant	1	0.24	—	—	0.24
	Open grown	1	0.68	—	—	0.68
	Dominant	33	0.82	0.13	0.75	2.74
	Codominant	57	0.86	0.11	0.81	4.30
	Intermediate	6	0.72	0.47	1.16	3.04
	Overtopped	2	1.79	1.70	2.40	3.48
	Dominant	2	0.41	0.14	0.19	0.54
	Codominant	3	0.06	0.03	0.06	0.12
	Intermediate	1	0.00	—	—	0.00
	Overtopped	1	0.03	—	—	0.03
Cestrum laurifolium L'Hér.	Codominant	1	0.14	—	—	0.14
	Dominant	1	0.02	—	—	0.02
	Codominant	1	0.16	—	—	0.16
Cinnamomum elongatum (Vahl ex Nees) Kosterm.	Dominant	5	0.58	0.24	0.53	1.48
	Codominant	10	0.85	0.17	0.55	1.74
	Intermediate	1	0.44	—	—	0.44
	Overtopped	3	0.31	0.17	0.30	0.62
C. montanum (Sw.) Bercht. & J. Presl	Codominant	1	1.42	—	—	1.42
	Codominant	1	0.04	—	—	0.04
Citharexylum spinosum L.	Open grown	1	0.32	—	—	0.32
	Dominant	1	0.50	—	—	0.50
	Codominant	12	0.17	0.03	0.11	0.34
	Intermediate	5	0.36	0.16	0.37	0.98
	Overtopped	4	0.03	0.01	0.03	0.06
Citrus ×paradisi Macfad. (pro sp.) [*maxima × sinensis*]	Codominant	3	0.09	0.03	0.05	0.14
	Dominant	1	0.00	—	—	0.00
	Codominant	5	0.10	0.05	0.11	0.22
	Intermediate	11	0.19	0.04	0.14	0.46
	Overtopped	10	0.05	0.01	0.03	0.11
Clibadium erosum (Sw.) DC.	Codominant	1	0.07	—	—	0.07
	Dominant	1	0.04	—	—	0.04

continued

Table A.1—Diameter at breast height (1.4 m) periodic annual increments (PAI, cm) by species and crown class with number of trees measured, standard error of the mean, standard deviation of the mean, and maximum observed PAI increase from Puerto Rico forest inventory data (continued)

| Species[a] | Crown class | N | Periodic annual increments | | | |
			Mean	SE	SD	Max
Cibadium erosum (Sw.) DC. (continued)	Codominant	1	0.16			0.16
	Intermediate	1	0.00			0.00
	Open grown	1	0.64			0.64
	Dominant	3	0.29	0.21	0.37	0.71
	Codominant	7	0.12	0.05	0.13	0.36
	Intermediate	3	0.07	0.05	0.08	0.16
	Overtopped	1	0.12			0.12
	Dominant	1	1.51			1.51
Coccoloba costata C. Wright ex Sauvalle	Intermediate	1	0.00			0.00
	Overtopped	3	0.03	0.02	0.04	0.07
	Dominant	4	0.18	0.12	0.25	0.54
	Codominant	9	0.16	0.05	0.16	0.44
	Intermediate	3	0.02	0.01	0.02	0.04
	Overtopped	2	0.00	0.00	0.00	0.00
	Codominant	8	0.02	0.01	0.03	0.10
C. microstachya Willd.	Dominant	2	0.11	0.05	0.07	0.16
	Codominant	15	0.09	0.02	0.08	0.30
	Intermediate	1	0.00			0.00
C. swartzii Meisn.	Codominant	1	0.31			0.31
	Intermediate	1	0.17			0.17
C. venosa L.	Intermediate	1	0.34			0.34
	Codominant	1	1.66			1.66
Cocos nucifera L.	Open grown	1	0.00			0.00
	Dominant	4	0.07	0.03	0.05	0.12
	Codominant	2	0.14	0.14	0.20	0.28
Coffea arabica L.	Codominant	1	0.12			0.12
	Intermediate	13	0.06	0.03	0.10	0.34
	Overtopped	16	0.02	0.01	0.04	0.10
	Codominant	5	0.25	0.10	0.23	0.53
	Overtopped	2	0.20	0.12	0.17	0.32
	Overtopped	1	0.14			0.14
Colubrina arborescens (Mill.) Sarg.	Intermediate	1	0.06			0.06
	Codominant	1	0.02			0.02
Conocarpus erectus L.	Codominant	2	0.47	0.47	0.66	0.94
	Intermediate	1	0.00			0.00
	Overtopped	1	0.06			0.06
Cordia alliodora (Ruiz & Pav.) Oken	Dominant	5	0.27	0.13	0.30	0.72
	Codominant	9	0.45	0.12	0.36	1.16
	Intermediate	2	0.26	0.10	0.14	0.36
	Overtopped	1	0.00			0.00
	Codominant	1	0.62			0.62

continued

Table A.1—Diameter at breast height (1.4 m) periodic annual increments (PAI, cm) by species and crown class with number of trees measured, standard error of the mean, standard deviation of the mean, and maximum observed PAI increase from Puerto Rico forest inventory data (continued)

| Species[1] | Crown class | N | Periodic annual increments | | | |
			Mean	SE	SD	Max
Cordia alliodora (Ruiz & Pav.) Oken (continued)	Intermediate	2	0.05	0.03	0.04	0.08
	Overtopped	1	0.22			0.22
C. sulcata DC.	Dominant	4	0.43	0.17	0.34	0.76
	Codominant	10	0.38	0.13	0.41	1.28
	Intermediate	4	1.60	1.16	2.32	5.08
	Overtopped	3	0.60	0.56	0.97	1.72
	Codominant	7	0.07	0.02	0.06	0.18
Croton astroites Dryand.	Intermediate	1	0.32			0.32
C. poecilanthus Urb.	Dominant	1	0.02			0.02
	Codominant	2	0.22	0.02	0.03	0.24
	Intermediate	3	0.05	0.03	0.05	0.10
Cupania americana L.	Dominant	1	0.68			0.68
	Codominant	5	0.67	0.14	0.32	1.00
	Intermediate	4	0.32	0.12	0.24	0.62
	Overtopped	2	0.78	0.10	0.14	0.88
	Dominant	1	0.04			0.04
	Codominant	1	0.36			0.36
	Codominant	2	0.52	0.52	0.74	1.04
	Intermediate	3	0.15	0.12	0.22	0.40
	Dominant	1	0.08			0.08
Dacryodes excelsa Vahl	Dominant	5	0.47	0.14	0.30	0.78
	Codominant	6	0.56	0.11	0.26	0.90
	Intermediate	1	0.18			0.18
	Overtopped	1	0.36			0.36
Daphnopsis americana (Mill.) J.R. Johnst.	Dominant	1	0.68			0.68
	Overtopped	1	0.28			0.28
Delonix regia (Bojer ex Hook.) Raf.	Codominant	3	1.03	0.24	0.42	1.42
	Dominant	4	0.86	0.72	1.45	3.03
	Codominant	11	0.43	0.19	0.65	2.28
	Intermediate	8	0.16	0.03	0.09	0.28
	Overtopped	6	0.16	0.08	0.20	0.56
Ditta myricoides Griseb.	Overtopped	2	0.11	0.01	0.01	0.12
	Intermediate	1	0.13			0.13
Drypetes glauca Vahl	Codominant	1	0.16			0.16
	Overtopped	2	0.14	0.02	0.03	0.16
	Codominant	2	0.06	0.02	0.03	0.08
	Intermediate	1	0.07			0.07
Erythrina berteriana Urb.	Dominant	1	0.10			0.10
	Codominant	1	0.64			0.64
E. poeppigiana (Walp.) O.F. Cook	Dominant	15	0.95	0.17	0.66	2.61
	Codominant	6	0.39	0.16	0.40	1.14

continued

11

Table A.1—Diameter at breast height (1.4 m) periodic annual increments (PAI, cm) by species and crown class with number of trees measured, standard error of the mean, standard deviation of the mean, and maximum observed PAI increase from Puerto Rico forest inventory data (continued)

Species[a]	Crown class	N	Periodic annual increments			
			Mean	SE	SD	Max
Erythrina poeppigiana (Walp.) O.F. Cook (continued)	Intermediate	6	0.56	0.32	0.78	2.10
	Overtopped	1	0.04			0.04
	Intermediate	3	0.07	0.03	0.05	0.12
	Overtopped	3	0.10	0.03	0.06	0.16
	Dominant	12	0.61	0.48	1.67	5.84
	Codominant	17	0.50	0.13	0.55	1.82
	Codominant	4	0.12	0.03	0.06	0.20
	Intermediate	6	0.06	0.01	0.04	0.10
	Overtopped	5	0.10	0.04	0.09	0.20
	Codominant	1	0.52			0.52
Eugenia confusa DC.	Intermediate	1	0.04			0.04
	Overtopped	1	0.14			0.14
	Dominant	1	0.38			0.38
E. ligustrina (Sw.) Willd.	Codominant	2	0.05	0.03	0.04	0.08
	Intermediate	1	0.00			0.00
E. monticola (Sw.) DC.	Codominant	4	0.13	0.05	0.10	0.24
	Intermediate	12	0.12	0.03	0.11	0.38
	Overtopped	5	0.03	0.02	0.05	0.12
E. pseudopsidium Jacq.	Dominant	2	0.57	0.09	0.13	0.66
	Codominant	1	0.00			0.00
	Intermediate	5	0.05	0.01	0.02	0.08
	Overtopped	1	0.10			0.10
E. xerophytica Britton	Codominant	2	0.07	0.05	0.07	0.12
Euphorbia cotinifolia L.	Codominant	1	0.00			0.00
	Dominant	2	0.11	0.01	0.01	0.12
	Codominant	7	0.09	0.02	0.06	0.18
	Intermediate	5	0.13	0.04	0.09	0.22
	Overtopped	2	0.04	0.04	0.06	0.08
	Overtopped	2	0.04	0.00	0.00	0.04
Ficus americana Aubl.	Codominant	1	0.65			0.65
	Dominant	2	1.71	1.35	1.90	3.05
	Codominant	5	0.25	0.13	0.29	0.61
	Intermediate	2	0.04	0.04	0.05	0.07
	Overtopped	1	0.13			0.13
F. trigonata L.	Dominant	1	0.18			0.18
	Codominant	1	0.10			0.10
	Codominant	3	0.20	0.16	0.28	0.52
Guaiacum officinale L.	Codominant	2	0.24	0.14	0.20	0.38
	Open grown	2	1.50	0.00	0.00	1.50
	Dominant	3	0.18	0.08	0.14	0.30
	Codominant	23	0.20	0.05	0.22	0.82

continued

Table A.1—Diameter at breast height (1.4 m) periodic annual increments (PAI, cm) by species and crown class with number of trees measured, standard error of the mean, standard deviation of the mean, and maximum observed PAI increase from Puerto Rico forest inventory data (continued)

Species[a]	Crown class	N	Periodic annual increments			
			Mean	SE	SD	Max
Guajacum officinale L. (continued)	Intermediate	7	0.26	0.07	0.19	0.56
	Overtopped	4	0.32	0.18	0.36	0.68
	Codominant	2	0.06	0.04	0.06	0.10
Guarea glabra Vahl	Intermediate	1	0.02			0.02
	Overtopped	3	0.02	0.02	0.03	0.06
G. guidonia (L.) Sleumer	Dominant	40	0.92	0.09	0.56	2.12
	Codominant	67	0.54	0.07	0.55	2.90
	Intermediate	52	0.53	0.07	0.49	2.04
	Overtopped	71	0.25	0.04	0.30	1.34
Guazuma ulmifolia Lam.	Open grown	1	0.42			0.42
	Dominant	5	0.82	0.26	0.58	1.80
	Codominant	11	0.44	0.11	0.36	1.18
	Intermediate	1	0.04			0.04
	Overtopped	1	0.28			0.28
Guettarda scabra (L.) Vent.	Dominant	3	0.04	0.01	0.02	0.06
	Codominant	15	0.06	0.02	0.07	0.28
	Intermediate	14	0.01	0.01	0.02	0.06
	Overtopped	9	0.01	0.01	0.02	0.04
Gymnda latifolia (Sw.) Urb.	Dominant	1	0.08			0.08
	Intermediate	2	0.11	0.05	0.07	0.16
	Overtopped	3	0.07	0.03	0.06	0.13
	Codominant	13	0.04	0.01	0.04	0.10
	Intermediate	8	0.05	0.01	0.03	0.08
	Overtopped	2	0.03	0.03	0.04	0.06
	Codominant	2	0.53	0.01	0.01	0.54
Henriettea squamulosum (Cogn.) W.S. Judd	Dominant	1	0.28			0.28
	Codominant	1	0.32			0.32
	Intermediate	2	0.06	0.06	0.08	0.12
	Intermediate	1	0.02			0.02
Hibiscus elatus Sw.	Overtopped	1	0.06			0.06
Hirtella rugosa Thuill. ex Pers.	Intermediate	2	0.04	0.04	0.06	0.08
	Codominant	7	0.21	0.08	0.21	0.68
	Intermediate	1	0.02			0.02
	Overtopped	1	0.14			0.14
	Dominant	6	0.36	0.06	0.14	0.62
	Codominant	7	0.31	0.06	0.16	0.62
	Intermediate	6	0.25	0.10	0.24	0.60
	Overtopped	3	0.10	0.04	0.07	0.18
Ilex nitida (Vahl) Maxim.	Intermediate	1	0.00			0.00
Inga laurina (Sw.) Willd.	Dominant	11	0.97	0.33	1.08	3.32
	Codominant	24	0.50	0.11	0.51	2.22

continued

Table A.1—Diameter at breast height (1.4 m) periodic annual increments (PAI, cm) by species and crown class with number of trees measured, standard error of the mean, standard deviation of the mean, and maximum observed PAI increase from Puerto Rico forest inventory data (continued)

| Species[a] | Crown class | N | Periodic annual increments | | | |
			Mean	SE	SD	Max
Inga laurina (Sw.) Willd. (continued)	Intermediate	9	0.36	0.15	0.44	1.44
	Overtopped	2	0.11	0.11	0.15	0.21
	Dominant	1	0.13			0.13
	Intermediate	1	0.54			0.54
	Dominant	24	0.62	0.10	0.48	2.18
	Codominant	46	0.42	0.08	0.54	2.54
	Intermediate	7	0.30	0.07	0.19	0.56
	Overtopped	10	0.37	0.12	0.37	1.26
Ixora ferrea (Jacq.) Benth.	Dominant	1	1.14			1.14
	Codominant	1	0.64			0.64
Krugiodendron ferreum (Vahl) Urb.	Codominant	4	0.11	0.06	0.12	0.28
	Intermediate	6	0.03	0.01	0.02	0.06
Laguncularia racemosa (L.) C.F. Gaertn.	Dominant	1	0.00			0.00
	Intermediate	4	0.15	0.04	0.07	0.24
	Overtopped	2	0.15	0.03	0.04	0.18
Leucaena leucocephala (Lam.) de Wit	Dominant	8	0.36	0.06	0.18	0.60
	Codominant	43	0.22	0.03	0.19	0.84
	Intermediate	12	0.10	0.02	0.07	0.20
	Overtopped	1	0.02			0.02
	Intermediate	1	0.18			0.18
Licaria parvifolia (Lam.) Kosterm.	Codominant	1	0.48			0.48
	Intermediate	1	0.00			0.00
	Overtopped	1	0.02			0.02
Lonchocarpus glaucifolius Urb.	Codominant	1	0.06			0.06
	Intermediate	1	0.10			0.10
L. heptaphyllus (Poir.) DC.	Dominant	2	0.18	0.05	0.06	0.22
	Codominant	1	0.36			0.36
	Dominant	1	0.90			0.90
	Codominant	1	0.15			0.15
Mammea americana L.	Dominant	1	1.11			1.11
	Codominant	1	0.31			0.31
	Overtopped	1	0.02			0.02
	Open grown	6	0.41	0.12	0.29	0.75
	Dominant	14	0.53	0.10	0.38	1.38
	Codominant	30	0.35	0.08	0.45	2.28
	Intermediate	6	0.29	0.15	0.37	0.94
	Overtopped	2	0.16	0.10	0.14	0.26
Manilkara bidentata (A. DC.) A. Chev	Dominant	1	1.05			1.05
	Codominant	1	0.61			0.61
Margaritaria nobilis L. f.	Codominant	1	0.02			0.02
	Intermediate	1	0.00			0.00

continued

Table A.1—Diameter at breast height (1.4 m) periodic annual increments (PAI, cm) by species and crown class with number of trees measured, standard error of the mean, standard deviation of the mean, and maximum observed PAI increase from Puerto Rico forest inventory data (continued)

Species[a]	Crown class	N	Periodic annual increments			
			Mean	SE	SD	Max
Margaritaria nobilis L. f. (continued)	Overtopped	1	0.08			0.08
Matayba domingensis (DC.) Radlk.	Dominant	1	0.12			0.12
	Codominant	2	0.12	0.04	0.06	0.16
Maytenus ponceana Britton	Intermediate	1	0.16			0.16
	Overtopped	1	0.00			0.00
	Codominant	8	0.63	0.13	0.37	1.16
	Intermediate	3	0.36	0.16	0.27	0.58
	Overtopped	2	0.11	0.01	0.01	0.12
	Dominant	1	0.22			0.22
	Codominant	5	0.11	0.03	0.07	0.22
	Intermediate	1	0.14			0.14
Miconia impetiolaris (Sw.) D. Don ex DC.	Dominant	1	0.49			0.49
	Intermediate	1	0.08			0.08
M. laevigata (L.) D. Don	Codominant	5	0.39	0.08	0.18	0.68
	Intermediate	2	0.34	0.14	0.20	0.48
	Dominant	1	0.02			0.02
	Codominant	2	0.63	0.12	0.16	0.74
	Intermediate	3	0.29	0.13	0.22	0.52
	Overtopped	5	0.08	0.06	0.13	0.30
M. pycnoneura Urb.	Overtopped	1	0.12			0.12
	Open grown	1	0.33			0.33
M. tetrandra (Sw.) D. Don	Dominant	1	0.10			0.10
	Codominant	1	0.12			0.12
	Intermediate	2	0.51	0.17	0.24	0.68
	Overtopped	1	0.50			0.50
	Dominant	5	0.05	0.01	0.03	0.10
	Codominant	8	0.16	0.09	0.25	0.72
	Dominant	1	0.05			0.05
	Codominant	21	0.18	0.03	0.13	0.46
	Intermediate	3	0.13	0.08	0.14	0.28
	Overtopped	1	0.15			0.15
Myrcia citrifolia (Aubl.) Urb.	Codominant	1	0.10			0.10
M. deflexa (Poir.) DC.	Codominant	1	0.31			0.31
	Intermediate	2	0.20	0.04	0.06	0.24
	Overtopped	2	0.06	0.00	0.01	0.06
M. fallax (Rich.) DC.	Intermediate	2	0.03	0.01	0.01	0.04
	Codominant	3	0.28	0.14	0.24	0.54
	Intermediate	7	0.33	0.10	0.26	0.62
	Overtopped	6	0.07	0.04	0.10	0.24
	Codominant	4	0.47	0.04	0.09	0.54
	Intermediate	1	0.32			0.32

continued

Table A.1—Diameter at breast height (1.4 m) periodic annual increments (PAI, cm) by species and crown class with number of trees measured, standard error of the mean, standard deviation of the mean, and maximum observed PAI increase from Puerto Rico forest inventory data (continued)

| Species[a] | Crown class | N | Periodic annual increments | | | |
			Mean	SE	SD	Max
Myrcia fallax (Rich.) DC. (continued)	Overtopped	1	0.16			0.16
	Dominant	1	0.34			0.34
	Codominant	3	0.43	0.07	0.12	0.52
	Intermediate	1	0.02			0.02
Nectandra coriacea (Sw.) Griseb.	Codominant	4	0.15	0.03	0.05	0.22
	Intermediate	2	0.36	0.04	0.06	0.40
	Overtopped	2	0.08	0.08	0.11	0.16
N. lihua (Ruiz & Pav.) Rohwer	Dominant	1	1.50			1.50
	Dominant	2	0.78	0.04	0.06	0.82
	Codominant	1	0.73			0.73
	Overtopped	2	0.08	0.02	0.03	0.10
Neea buxifolia (Hook. f.) Heimerl	Intermediate	1	0.02			0.02
Neolaugeria resinosa (Vahl) Nicolson	Dominant	1	0.70			0.70
	Codominant	12	0.27	0.07	0.24	0.70
	Intermediate	8	0.24	0.08	0.22	0.74
	Overtopped	2	0.11	0.09	0.13	0.20
Ocotea floribunda (Sw.) Mez	Dominant	1	0.34			0.34
	Codominant	1	0.28			0.28
	Dominant	4	0.46	0.07	0.15	0.61
	Codominant	15	0.25	0.05	0.21	0.66
	Intermediate	11	0.17	0.08	0.26	0.76
	Overtopped	11	0.26	0.09	0.29	0.78
O. moschata (Pav. ex Meisn.) Mez	Dominant	1	0.52			0.52
	Codominant	1	0.18			0.18
O. wrightii (Meisn.) Mez	Dominant	1	0.58			0.58
Ormosia krugii Urb.	Dominant	2	0.28	0.04	0.06	0.32
	Codominant	9	0.22	0.07	0.22	0.66
	Intermediate	3	0.07	0.03	0.05	0.12
	Overtopped	1	0.00			0.00
Ouratea littoralis Urb.	Intermediate	1	0.08			0.08
	Open grown	1	5.74			5.74
	Codominant	4	0.04	0.03	0.06	0.12
Palicourea croceoides Ham.	Codominant	3	0.07	0.02	0.04	0.11
	Overtopped	2	0.11	0.03	0.04	0.13
	Open grown	1	0.58			0.58
Peltophorum pterocarpum (DC.) Backer ex K. Heyne	Codominant	5	0.64	0.04	0.09	0.72
	Dominant	1	0.60			0.60
	Codominant	5	0.64	0.31	0.70	1.80
	Intermediate	3	1.26	0.52	0.90	2.28
	Dominant	1	0.20			0.20

continued

Table A.1—Diameter at breast height (1.4 m) periodic annual increments (PAI, cm) by species and crown class with number of trees measured, standard error of the mean, standard deviation of the mean, and maximum observed PAI increase from Puerto Rico forest inventory data (continued)

Species[a]	Crown class	N	Periodic annual increments			
			Mean	SE	SD	Max
Peltophorum pterocarpum (DC.) Backer ex K. Heyne (continued)	Codominant	3	0.21	0.04	0.08	0.28
	Intermediate	1	0.30			0.30
	Overtopped	1	0.06			0.06
Picramnia pentandra Sw.	Intermediate	1	0.08			0.08
	Dominant	1	0.14			0.14
	Codominant	12	0.05	0.02	0.06	0.16
	Intermediate	1	0.00			0.00
	Overtopped	2	0.13	0.03	0.04	0.16
Pilosocereus royenii (L.) Byles & Rowley	Codominant	2	0.32	0.30	0.42	0.62
	Codominant	7	0.28	0.08	0.22	0.66
Piper aduncum L.	Intermediate	1	0.15			0.15
	Codominant	2	0.05	0.01	0.01	0.06
	Intermediate	3	0.25	0.16	0.27	0.56
	Intermediate	1	0.14			0.14
Pithecellobium dulce (Roxb.) Benth.	Dominant	1	2.06			2.06
	Codominant	4	1.53	0.47	0.94	2.74
Plumeria obtusa L.	Codominant	3	0.21	0.02	0.04	0.24
Podocarpus coriaceus Rich.	Codominant	1	0.05			0.05
Poitea florida (Vahl) Lavin	Dominant	1	0.04			0.04
Pouteria multiflora (A. DC.) Eyma	Dominant	5	0.66	0.59	1.31	3.00
	Codominant	2	0.22	0.20	0.29	0.42
	Overtopped	2	0.54	0.00	0.00	0.54
P. sapota (Jacq.) H.E. Moore & Stearn	Dominant	1	0.24			0.24
	Codominant	1	0.46			0.46
Prestoea acuminata (Willd.) H.E. Moore var. *montana* (Graham) A. Hend. & G. Galeano	Dominant	7	0.02	0.01	0.03	0.08
	Codominant	34	0.04	0.01	0.06	0.20
	Intermediate	27	0.16	0.03	0.18	0.74
	Overtopped	20	0.19	0.05	0.25	1.00
Prosopis pallida (Humb. & Bonpl. ex Willd.) Kunth	Codominant	3	0.11	0.11	0.18	0.32
Prunus myrtifolia (L.) Urb.	Overtopped	1	0.09			0.09
Pseudolmedia spuria (Sw.) Griseb.	Codominant	1	0.18			0.18
Psidium amplexicaule Pers.	Intermediate	1	0.05			0.05
	Overtopped	4	0.07	0.03	0.07	0.16
P. guajava L.	Codominant	6	0.07	0.05	0.12	0.31
	Intermediate	3	0.04	0.02	0.03	0.06
	Overtopped	2	0.00	0.00	0.00	0.00
Psychotria berteriana DC.	Overtopped	1	0.04			0.04

continued

Table A.1—Diameter at breast height (1.4 m) periodic annual increments (PAL, cm) by species and crown class with number of trees measured, standard error of the mean, standard deviation of the mean, and maximum observed PAI increase from Puerto Rico forest inventory data (continued)

| Species[a] | Crown class | N | Periodic annual increments | | | |
			Mean	SE	SD	Max
Psychotria brachiata Sw.	Overtopped	2	0.01	0.01	0.01	0.02
Quararibea turbinata (Sw.) Poir.	Intermediate	4	0.21	0.07	0.15	0.40
	Overtopped	3	0.08	0.03	0.05	0.12
Randia aculeata L.	Codominant	3	0.17	0.04	0.08	0.26
	Intermediate	1	0.24			0.24
	Overtopped	1	0.08			0.08
Rhizophora mangle L.	Dominant	1	0.00			0.00
	Codominant	1	0.00			0.00
	Intermediate	1	0.00			0.00
Roystonea borinquena O.F. Cook	Open grown	1	0.00			0.00
	Dominant	10	0.25	0.13	0.42	1.25
	Codominant	6	0.46	0.21	0.52	1.28
	Intermediate	2	3.40	0.60	0.85	4.00
	Overtopped	1	0.44			0.44
Sagraea umbrosa (Sw.) DC.	Dominant	3	0.20	0.04	0.07	0.27
	Codominant	2	0.20	0.09	0.12	0.28
	Intermediate	1	0.45			0.45
Samanea saman (Jacq.) Merr.	Codominant	1	2.30			2.30
Sapindus saponaria L.	Codominant	1	0.25			0.25
Sapium laurocerasus Desf.	Codominant	1	0.34			0.34
	Intermediate	1	0.88			0.88
Savia sessiliflora (Sw.) Willd.	Overtopped	2	0.06	0.04	0.06	0.10
Schefflera morototoni (Aubl.) Maguire, Steyerm. & Frodin	Open grown	1	0.32			0.32
	Dominant	5	0.41	0.11	0.25	0.72
	Codominant	18	0.33	0.06	0.27	0.88
	Intermediate	4	0.82	0.35	0.70	1.70
	Overtopped	3	0.21	0.04	0.06	0.28
Schoepfia obovata C. Wright	Codominant	1	0.00			0.00
Senna siamea (Lam.) Irwin & Barneby	Codominant	7	0.66	0.27	0.70	2.02
	Intermediate	2	0.98	0.50	0.71	1.48
Sideroxylon cubense (Griseb.) T.D. Penn.	Codominant	1	0.02			0.02
	Intermediate	1	0.11			0.11
S. salicifolium (L.) Lam.	Codominant	7	0.22	0.05	0.15	0.41
	Intermediate	2	0.08	0.04	0.06	0.12
Sloanea berteriana Choisy ex DC.	Dominant	1	0.22			0.22
	Codominant	4	0.13	0.02	0.05	0.20
	Intermediate	5	0.05	0.02	0.04	0.10
Solanum rugosum Dunal	Overtopped	2	0.09	0.09	0.13	0.18

continued

18

Table A.1—Diameter at breast height (1.4 m) periodic annual increments (PAI, cm) by species and crown class with number of trees measured, standard error of the mean, standard deviation of the mean, and maximum observed PAI increase from Puerto Rico forest inventory data (continued)

Species[a]	Crown class	N	Periodic annual increments			
			Mean	SE	SD	Max
Spathodea campanulata P. Beauv.	Dominant	46	0.95	0.10	0.66	3.24
	Codominant	137	0.77	0.06	0.67	3.76
	Intermediate	79	0.44	0.05	0.44	2.14
	Overtopped	69	0.22	0.03	0.28	1.46
Spondias dulcis Parkinson	Dominant	1	0.47			0.47
	Codominant	1	0.00			0.00
S. mombin L.	Dominant	6	0.64	0.12	0.30	1.02
	Codominant	7	0.59	0.16	0.43	1.18
	Intermediate	3	0.35	0.07	0.12	0.43
Swietenia macrophylla King	Codominant	3	0.33	0.20	0.34	0.72
S. mahagoni (L.) Jacq.	Dominant	3	0.27	0.13	0.23	0.48
	Codominant	7	0.16	0.05	0.13	0.30
	Intermediate	1	0.16			0.16
Symplocos martinicensis Jacq.	Codominant	4	0.39	0.11	0.22	0.64
Syzygium jambos (L.) Alston	Dominant	2	0.00	0.00	0.00	0.00
	Codominant	27	0.12	0.03	0.14	0.54
	Intermediate	30	0.15	0.04	0.20	0.90
	Overtopped	26	0.10	0.04	0.18	0.70
Tabebuia haemantha (Bertol. ex Spreng.) DC.	Dominant	1	0.12			0.12
	Codominant	5	0.03	0.02	0.05	0.12
	Intermediate	1	0.04			0.04
	Overtopped	1	0.02			0.02
T. heterophylla (DC.) Britton	Dominant	27	0.27	0.05	0.25	0.84
	Codominant	50	0.38	0.06	0.39	1.46
	Intermediate	22	0.20	0.05	0.23	0.78
	Overtopped	12	0.08	0.02	0.08	0.30
T. rigida Urb.	Codominant	1	0.00			0.00
Tamarindus indica L.	Open grown	1	1.52			1.52
	Codominant	1	1.08			1.08
Terminalia catappa L.	Dominant	5	0.61	0.08	0.19	0.83
	Codominant	1	0.68			0.68
	Intermediate	1	0.42			0.42
Tetragastris balsamifera (Sw.) Oken	Dominant	1	0.08			0.08
	Codominant	3	0.38	0.16	0.28	0.60
	Intermediate	2	0.29	0.01	0.01	0.30
	Overtopped	1	0.80			0.80
Tetrazygia elaeagnoides (Sw.) DC.	Codominant	11	0.21	0.08	0.27	0.96
	Intermediate	4	0.19	0.06	0.11	0.34
	Overtopped	3	0.07	0.05	0.08	0.16

continued

Table A.1—Diameter at breast height (1.4 m) periodic annual increments (PAI, cm) by species and crown class with number of trees measured, standard error of the mean, standard deviation of the mean, and maximum observed PAI increase from Puerto Rico forest inventory data (continued)

Species[a]	Crown class	N	Mean	SE	SD	Max
			\multicolumn{4}{c}{Periodic annual increments}
Thespesia grandiflora DC.	Dominant	3	0.20	0.08	0.14	0.36
	Codominant	6	0.38	0.16	0.39	1.14
	Intermediate	3	0.11	0.05	0.08	0.20
	Overtopped	1	0.22			0.22
Thouinia striata Radlk.	Dominant	1	0.84			0.84
	Codominant	9	0.10	0.04	0.13	0.38
	Intermediate	5	0.19	0.09	0.19	0.50
T. striata Radlk. var. *portoricensis* (Radlk.) Votava & Alain	Dominant	2	0.06	0.00	0.00	0.06
	Codominant	5	0.02	0.02	0.04	0.10
	Intermediate	5	0.02	0.02	0.03	0.08
Trema micrantha (L.) Blume	Codominant	1	0.54			0.54
	Overtopped	1	0.06			0.06
Trichilia hirta L.	Codominant	2	0.50	0.24	0.34	0.74
	Overtopped	1	0.00			0.00
T. pallida Sw.	Intermediate	3	0.25	0.10	0.18	0.44
	Overtopped	9	0.05	0.02	0.05	0.16
Turpinia occidentalis (Sw.) G. Don	Codominant	10	0.26	0.09	0.27	0.78
	Overtopped	1	0.01			0.01
Urera baccifera (L.) Gaudich.	Overtopped	1	0.04			0.04
Vitex divaricata Sw.	Codominant	4	0.31	0.17	0.34	0.76
	Intermediate	1	0.12			0.12
Xylosma buxifolia A. Gray	Intermediate	1	0.05			0.05
X. pachyphylla (Krug & Urb.) Urb.	Codominant	1	0.14			0.14
Zanthoxylum martinicense (Lam.) DC.	Dominant	8	0.84	0.29	0.82	2.62
	Codominant	15	0.43	0.09	0.35	1.38
	Intermediate	3	0.31	0.11	0.19	0.48
	Overtopped	5	0.21	0.09	0.19	0.42
Z. monophyllum (Lam.) P. Wilson	Codominant	2	0.36	0.12	0.17	0.48
	Overtopped	2	0.03	0.01	0.01	0.04

— = insufficient sample; N = number of trees measured; SE = standard error of the mean; SD = standard deviation of the mean; Max = maximum observed.

[a] USDA Natural Resources Conservation Service (2006).

Table A.2—Diameter at breast height (1.4 m) periodic annual increments (PAI, cm) by species and crown position, with number of trees measured, standard error of the mean, standard deviation of the mean, and maximum observed PAI increase from Puerto Rico forest inventory data

Species[a]	Crown position[b]	N	Periodic annual increments			
			Mean	SE	SD	Max
Acacia farnesiana (L.) Willd.	Overstory	5	0.50	0.15	0.34	0.86
	All	5	0.50	0.15	0.34	0.86
Acrocomia media O.F. Cook	Overstory	1	0.04			0.04
	All	1	0.04			0.04
Adelia ricinella L.	Understory	1	0.02			0.02
	All	1	0.02			0.02
Adenanthera pavonina L.	Overstory	7	1.15	0.16	0.42	1.86
	Understory	16	0.33	0.12	0.47	1.48
	All	23	0.58	0.12	0.59	1.86
Albizia procera (Roxb.) Benth.	Overstory	27	0.71	0.12	0.63	2.22
	Understory	3	0.11	0.04	0.06	0.16
	All	30	0.65	0.11	0.62	2.22
Alchornea latifolia Sw.	Overstory	13	0.27	0.07	0.27	1.04
	Understory	9	0.21	0.04	0.13	0.46
	All	38	0.27	0.04	0.23	1.04
Alsophila portoricensis (Spreng. ex Kuhn) Conant	Understory	1	0.00			0.00
	All	1	0.00			0.00
Amyris elemifera L.	Overstory	8	0.14	0.04	0.13	0.42
	Understory	12	0.04	0.01	0.04	0.10
	All	21	0.08	0.02	0.10	0.42
Andira inermis (W. Wright) Kunth ex DC.	Overstory	88	0.24	0.03	0.25	1.26
	Understory	44	0.14	0.03	0.20	0.80
	All	169	0.23	0.02	0.25	1.26
Annona muricata L.	Overstory	2	0.25	0.23	0.33	0.48
	Understory	2	0.36	0.24	0.34	0.60
	All	4	0.31	0.14	0.28	0.60
A. reticulata L.	Overstory	2	0.09	0.09	0.13	0.18
	All	2	0.09	0.09	0.13	0.18
A. squamosa L.	Overstory	2	0.46	0.46	0.65	0.92
	All	2	0.46	0.46	0.65	0.92
Antirhea obtusifolia Urb.	Understory	1	0.16			0.16
	All	1	0.16			0.16
Ardisia obovata Desv. ex Ham.	Overstory	11	0.09	0.03	0.09	0.28
	Understory	11	0.07	0.02	0.07	0.24
	All	27	0.07	0.01	0.07	0.28
Artocarpus altilis (Parkinson) Fosberg	Overstory	14	0.25	0.05	0.19	0.68
	Understory	5	0.17	0.08	0.18	0.44
	All	29	0.23	0.04	0.23	0.81

continued

21

Table A.2—Diameter at breast height (1.4 m) periodic annual increments (PAI, cm) by species and crown position, with number of trees measured, standard error of the mean, standard deviation of the mean, and maximum observed PAI increase from Puerto Rico forest inventory data (continued)

Species[a]	Crown position[b]	N	Periodic annual increments			
			Mean	SE	SD	Max
Avicennia germinans (L.) L.	Overstory	14	0.23	0.11	0.40	1.20
	Understory	1	0.10			0.10
	All	15	0.22	0.10	0.39	1.20
Banara portoricensis Krug & Urb.	Understory	1	0.32			0.32
	All	1	0.28			0.28
Beilschmiedia pendula (Sw.) Hemsl.	Overstory	1	0.34			0.34
	All	1	0.34			0.34
Bourreria succulenta Jacq.	Overstory	28	0.15	0.04	0.23	0.98
	Understory	6	0.10	0.06	0.14	0.32
	All	34	0.14	0.04	0.22	0.98
B. virgata (Sw.) G. Don	Understory	2	0.10	0.02	0.03	0.12
	All	3	0.08	0.02	0.04	0.12
Buchenavia tetraphylla (Aubl.) Howard	Overstory	6	0.71	0.18	0.44	1.45
	Understory	1	0.04			0.04
	All	7	0.62	0.18	0.48	1.45
Bucida buceras L.	Overstory	12	0.32	0.05	0.18	0.60
	Understory	1	0.00			0.00
	All	15	0.34	0.07	0.27	1.06
Bursera simaruba (L.) Sarg.	Overstory	62	0.36	0.05	0.40	2.48
	Understory	4	0.05	0.03	0.06	0.12
	All	67	0.34	0.05	0.40	2.48
Byrsonima lucida (Mill.) DC.	Overstory	6	0.10	0.03	0.07	0.22
	All	6	0.10	0.03	0.07	0.22
B. spicata (Cav.) Kunth	Overstory	11	0.49	0.13	0.42	1.56
	Understory	2	0.36	0.16	0.23	0.52
	All	19	0.44	0.09	0.39	1.56
B. wadsworthii Little	Understory	1	0.02			0.02
	All	1	0.02			0.02
Calophyllum antillanum Britton	Overstory	19	0.48	0.08	0.36	1.38
	Understory	8	0.28	0.09	0.25	0.80
	All	41	0.41	0.05	0.32	1.38
Canella winterana (L.) Gaertn.	Overstory	3	0.13	0.02	0.03	0.16
	Understory	1	0.16			0.16
	All	4	0.14	0.01	0.03	0.16
Capparis baducca L.	Understory	2	0.02	0.02	0.03	0.04
	All	2	0.02	0.02	0.03	0.04
C. cynophallophora L.	Overstory	1	0.08			0.08
	All	1	0.08			0.08

continued

Table A.2—Diameter at breast height (1.4 m) periodic annual increments (PAI, cm) by species and crown position, with number of trees measured, standard error of the mean, standard deviation of the mean, and maximum observed PAI increase from Puerto Rico forest inventory data (continued)

| Species[a] | Crown position[b] | N | Periodic annual increments | | | |
			Mean	SE	SD	Max
Capparis flexuosa (L.) L.	Understory	2	0.02	0.02	0.03	0.04
	All	2	0.02	0.02	0.03	0.04
C. hastata Jacq.	Overstory	4	0.05	0.04	0.08	0.16
	Understory	2	0.03	0.01	0.01	0.04
	All	6	0.04	0.02	0.06	0.16
Carapa guianensis Aubl.	Overstory	1	0.10			0.10
	All	1	0.10			0.10
Casearia arborea (Rich.) Urb.	Overstory	5	0.25	0.09	0.20	0.48
	Understory	17	0.17	0.04	0.15	0.48
	All	32	0.20	0.03	0.16	0.49
C. decandra Jacq.	Understory	13	0.03	0.01	0.03	0.10
	All	17	0.03	0.01	0.03	0.10
C. guianensis (Aubl.) Urb.	Overstory	8	0.17	0.05	0.14	0.42
	Understory	64	0.10	0.01	0.12	0.50
	All	99	0.11	0.01	0.11	0.50
C. sylvestris Sw.	Overstory	5	0.19	0.09	0.19	0.52
	Understory	42	0.10	0.02	0.12	0.48
	All	67	0.11	0.02	0.13	0.56
Cassine xylocarpa Vent.	Overstory	5	0.03	0.02	0.04	0.10
	All	5	0.03	0.02	0.04	0.10
Castilla elastica Sess	Overstory	1	0.24			0.24
	All	3	0.82	0.68	1.17	2.17
Cecropia schreberiana Miq.	Overstory	76	0.84	0.09	0.81	4.30
	Understory	8	0.91	0.52	1.46	3.48
	All	137	0.80	0.07	0.77	4.30
Cedrela odorata L.	Overstory	5	0.13	0.05	0.11	0.28
	Understory	2	0.02	0.02	0.02	0.03
	All	11	0.18	0.05	0.18	0.54
Cestrum laurifolium L'Hér.	Overstory	1	0.14			0.14
	All	1	0.14			0.14
Chrysophyllum cainito L.	Overstory	2	0.09	0.07	0.10	0.16
	All	2	0.09	0.07	0.10	0.16
Cinnamomum elongatum (Vahl ex Nees) Kosterm.	Overstory	15	0.76	0.14	0.54	1.74
	Understory	4	0.34	0.13	0.25	0.62
	All	26	0.60	0.09	0.48	1.74
C. montanum (Sw.) Bercht. & J. Presl	Overstory	1	1.42			1.42
	All	1	1.42			1.42
Citharexylum caudatum L.	Overstory	1	0.04			0.04
	All	1	0.04			0.04

continued

Table A.2—Diameter at breast height (1.4 m) periodic annual increments (PAI, cm) by species and crown position, with number of trees measured, standard error of the mean, standard deviation of the mean, and maximum observed PAI increase from Puerto Rico forest inventory data (continued)

Species[a]	Crown position[b]	N	Periodic annual increments			
			Mean	SE	SD	Max
Citharexylum spinosum L.	Overstory	14	0.20	0.04	0.14	0.50
	Understory	9	0.22	0.10	0.31	0.98
	All	23	0.21	0.05	0.22	0.98
Citrus ×paradisi Macfad. (pro sp.) [*maxima × sinensis*]	Overstory	3	0.09	0.03	0.05	0.14
	All	3	0.09	0.03	0.05	0.14
C. ×sinensis (L.) Osbeck (pro sp.) [*maxima × reticulata*]	Overstory	6	0.08	0.04	0.10	0.22
	Understory	21	0.07	0.01	0.07	0.24
	All	38	0.13	0.03	0.21	1.19
Clibadium erosum (Sw.) DC.	Overstory	1	0.07	—	—	0.07
	All	1	0.07	—	—	0.07
Clusia clusioides (Griseb.) D'Arcy	Overstory	2	0.10	0.06	0.08	0.16
	Understory	1	0.00	—	—	0.00
	All	3	0.07	0.05	0.08	0.16
C. rosea Jacq.	Overstory	8	0.18	0.08	0.22	0.64
	Understory	4	0.08	0.04	0.07	0.16
	All	23	0.29	0.07	0.31	0.98
Cnemidaria horrida (L.) C. Presl	Overstory	1	1.51	—	—	1.51
	All	1	1.51	—	—	1.51
Coccoloba costata C. Wright ex Sauvalle	Understory	4	0.02	0.02	0.03	0.07
	All	4	0.02	0.02	0.03	0.07
C. diversifolia Jacq.	Overstory	13	0.17	0.05	0.18	0.54
	Understory	5	0.01	0.01	0.02	0.04
	All	23	0.12	0.03	0.16	0.54
C. krugii Lindau	Overstory	8	0.02	0.01	0.03	0.10
	All	8	0.02	0.01	0.03	0.10
C. microstachya Willd.	Overstory	17	0.09	0.02	0.08	0.30
	All	18	0.11	0.02	0.09	0.31
C. pyrifolia Desf.	Understory	1	0.00	—	—	0.00
	All	1	0.00	—	—	0.00
C. swartzii Meisn.	Overstory	1	0.31	—	—	0.31
	Understory	1	0.17	—	—	0.17
	All	2	0.24	0.07	0.10	0.31
C. venosa L.	Understory	1	0.34	—	—	0.34
	All	1	0.34	—	—	0.34
Cochlospermum vitifolium (Willd.) Willd. ex Spreng.	Overstory	1	1.66	—	—	1.66
	All	1	1.66	—	—	1.66
Cocos nucifera L.	Overstory	6	0.09	0.04	0.10	0.28
	All	7	0.08	0.04	0.10	0.28

continued

Table A.2—Diameter at breast height (1.4 m) periodic annual increments (PAI, cm) by species and crown position, with number of trees measured, standard error of the mean, standard deviation of the mean, and maximum observed PAI increase from Puerto Rico forest inventory data (continued)

Species[a]	Crown position[b]	N	Periodic annual increments			
			Mean	SE	SD	Max
Coffea arabica L.	Overstory	1	0.12			0.12
	Understory	29	0.04	0.01	0.08	0.34
	All	36	0.06	0.02	0.10	0.38
C. liberica W. Bull ex Hiern.	Overstory	5	0.25	0.10	0.23	0.53
	Understory	2	0.20	0.12	0.17	0.32
	All	9	0.28	0.06	0.19	0.53
Cojoba arborea (L.) Britton & Rose	Understory	1	0.14			0.14
	All	1	0.14			0.14
Colubrina arborescens (Mill.) Sarg.	Understory	1	0.06			0.06
	All	1	0.06			0.06
Comocladia dodonaea (L.) Urb.	Overstory	1	0.02			0.02
	All	1	0.02			0.02
Conocarpus erectus L.	Overstory	2	0.47	0.47	0.66	0.94
	Understory	2	0.03	0.03	0.04	0.06
	All	4	0.25	0.23	0.46	0.94
Cordia alliodora (Ruiz & Pav.) Oken	Overstory	12	0.45	0.09	0.33	1.16
	Understory	2	0.26	0.10	0.14	0.36
	All	26	0.32	0.06	0.30	1.16
C. borinquensis Urb.	Overstory	1	0.62			0.62
	Understory	3	0.11	0.06	0.10	0.22
	All	5	0.26	0.10	0.22	0.51
C. sulcata DC.	Overstory	14	0.40	0.10	0.38	1.28
	Understory	6	1.36	0.78	1.91	5.08
	All	31	0.56	0.17	0.94	5.08
Crossopetalum rhacoma Crantz	Overstory	7	0.07	0.02	0.06	0.18
	All	7	0.07	0.02	0.06	0.18
Croton astroites Dryand.	Understory	1	0.32			0.32
	All	1	0.32			0.32
C. poecilanthus Urb.	Overstory	3	0.15	0.07	0.12	0.24
	Understory	3	0.05	0.03	0.05	0.10
	All	6	0.10	0.04	0.10	0.24
Cupania americana L.	Overstory	6	0.67	0.12	0.28	1.00
	Understory	6	0.47	0.13	0.31	0.88
	All	21	0.48	0.07	0.31	1.00
C. triquetra A. Rich.	Overstory	2	0.20	0.16	0.23	0.36
	All	2	0.20	0.16	0.23	0.36
Cyathea arborea (L.) Sm.	Overstory	2	0.52	0.52	0.74	1.04
	Understory	3	0.15	0.12	0.22	0.40
	All	9	0.18	0.12	0.35	1.04

continued

Table A.2—Diameter at breast height (1.4 m) periodic annual increments (PAI, cm) by species and crown position, with number of trees measured, standard error of the mean, standard deviation of the mean, and maximum observed PAI increase from Puerto Rico forest inventory data (continued)

Species[a]	Crown position[b]	N	Periodic annual increments			
			Mean	SE	SD	Max
Cyrilla racemiflora L.	Overstory	1	0.08			0.08
	All	1	0.08			0.08
Dacryodes excelsa Vahl	Overstory	10	0.53	0.09	0.28	0.90
	Understory	2	0.27	0.09	0.13	0.36
	All	19	0.46	0.07	0.28	1.08
Daphnopsis americana (Mill.) J.R. Johnst.	Overstory	1	0.68			0.68
	Understory	1	0.28			0.28
	All	2	0.48	0.20	0.28	0.68
Delonix regia (Bojer ex Hook.) Raf.	Overstory	3	1.03	0.24	0.42	1.42
	All	3	1.03	0.24	0.42	1.42
Dendropanax arboreus (L.) Decne. & Planch. ex Britton	Overstory	13	0.37	0.17	0.61	2.28
	Understory	14	0.16	0.04	0.14	0.56
	All	51	0.35	0.08	0.58	3.03
Ditta myricoides Griseb.	Understory	2	0.11	0.01	0.01	0.12
	All	2	0.11	0.01	0.01	0.12
Drypetes alba Poit.	Understory	1	0.13			0.13
	All	1	0.13			0.13
D. glauca Vahl	Overstory	1	0.16			0.16
	Understory	2	0.14	0.02	0.03	0.16
	All	3	0.15	0.01	0.02	0.16
Erithalis fruticosa L.	Overstory	2	0.06	0.02	0.03	0.08
	Understory	1	0.07			0.07
	All	3	0.06	0.01	0.02	0.08
Erythrina bertertana Urb.	Overstory	2	0.37	0.27	0.38	0.64
	All	2	0.37	0.27	0.38	0.64
E. poeppigiana (Walp.) O.F. Cook	Overstory	21	0.76	0.14	0.65	2.61
	Understory	7	0.20	0.07	0.19	0.52
	All	34	0.73	0.12	0.71	2.61
Erythroxylum rotundifolium Lunan	Understory	6	0.09	0.02	0.05	0.16
	All	6	0.09	0.02	0.05	0.16
Eucalyptus robusta Sm.	Overstory	29	0.54	0.21	1.13	5.84
	All	29	0.54	0.21	1.13	5.84
Eugenia biflora (L.) DC.	Overstory	4	0.12	0.03	0.06	0.20
	Understory	11	0.08	0.02	0.07	0.20
	All	16	0.08	0.02	0.07	0.20
E. boqueronensis Britton	Overstory	1	0.52			0.52
	All	1	0.52			0.52
E. confusa DC.	Understory	2	0.09	0.05	0.07	0.14
	All	2	0.09	0.05	0.07	0.14

continued

Table A.2—Diameter at breast height (1.4 m) periodic annual increments (PAI, cm) by species and crown position, with number of trees measured, standard error of the mean, standard deviation of the mean, and maximum observed PAI increase from Puerto Rico forest inventory data (continued)

Species[a]	Crown position[b]	N	Periodic annual increments			
			Mean	SE	SD	Max
Eugenia domingensis Berg	Overstory	1	0.38	—	—	0.38
	All	1	0.38	—	—	0.38
E. ligustrina (Sw.) Willd.	Overstory	2	0.05	0.03	0.04	0.08
	Understory	1	0.00	—	—	0.00
	All	3	0.03	0.02	0.04	0.08
E. monticola (Sw.) DC.	Overstory	4	0.13	0.05	0.10	0.24
	Understory	17	0.09	0.02	0.10	0.38
	All	24	0.12	0.02	0.11	0.38
E. pseudopsidium Jacq.	Overstory	2	0.57	0.09	0.13	0.66
	All	2	0.57	0.09	0.13	0.66
E. rhombea (Berg) Krug & Urb.	Overstory	1	0.00	—	—	0.00
	Understory	6	0.06	0.01	0.03	0.10
	All	7	0.05	0.01	0.03	0.10
E. xerophytica Britton	Overstory	2	0.07	0.05	0.07	0.12
	All	2	0.07	0.05	0.07	0.12
Euphorbia cotinifolia L.	Overstory	1	0.00	—	—	0.00
	All	1	0.00	—	—	0.00
Exostema caribaeum (Jacq.) Schult.	Overstory	9	0.09	0.02	0.05	0.18
	All	9	0.09	0.02	0.05	0.18
Exothea paniculata (Juss.) Radlk.	Understory	5	0.13	0.04	0.09	0.22
	All	8	0.12	0.03	0.10	0.25
Faramea occidentalis (L.) A. Rich.	Understory	2	0.04	0.00	0.00	0.04
	All	2	0.04	0.00	0.00	0.04
Ficus americana Aubl.	Overstory	1	0.65	—	—	0.65
	All	1	0.65	—	—	0.65
F. citrifolia Mill.	Overstory	7	0.23	0.10	0.26	0.61
	Understory	3	0.49	0.43	0.74	1.35
	All	16	0.58	0.21	0.83	3.05
F. trigonata L.	Overstory	2	0.14	0.04	0.06	0.18
	All	2	0.14	0.04	0.06	0.18
Gliricidia sepium (Jacq.) Kunth ex Walp.	Overstory	3	0.20	0.16	0.28	0.52
	All	3	0.20	0.16	0.28	0.52
Guajacum officinale L.	Overstory	2	0.24	0.14	0.20	0.38
	All	2	0.24	0.14	0.20	0.38
Guapira fragrans (Dum. Cours.) Little	Overstory	26	0.20	0.04	0.21	0.82
	Understory	11	0.28	0.07	0.24	0.68
	All	44	0.28	0.05	0.34	1.50
G. obtusata (Jacq.) Little	Overstory	2	0.06	0.04	0.06	0.10
	All	2	0.06	0.04	0.06	0.10

continued

Table A.2—Diameter at breast height (1.4 m) periodic annual increments (PAI, cm) by species and crown position, with number of trees measured, standard error of the mean, standard deviation of the mean, and maximum observed PAI increase from Puerto Rico forest inventory data (continued)

Species[a]	Crown position[b]	N	Periodic annual increments			
			Mean	SE	SD	Max
Guarea glabra Vahl	Understory	3	0.03	0.02	0.03	0.06
	All	4	0.02	0.01	0.03	0.06
G. guidonia (L.) Sleumer	Overstory	107	0.58	0.05	0.54	2.90
	Understory	123	0.37	0.04	0.41	2.04
	All	352	0.54	0.03	0.53	2.90
Guazuma ulmifolia Lam.	Overstory	16	0.56	0.11	0.45	1.80
	Understory	1	0.04			0.04
	All	21	0.53	0.09	0.42	1.80
Guettarda scabra (L.) Vent.	Overstory	18	0.05	0.02	0.07	0.28
	Understory	15	0.02	0.01	0.02	0.06
	All	47	0.03	0.01	0.05	0.28
Gyminda latifolia (Sw.) Urb.	Overstory	1	0.08			0.08
	Understory	4	0.09	0.03	0.06	0.16
	All	7	0.08	0.02	0.05	0.16
Gymnanthes lucida Sw.	Overstory	13	0.04	0.01	0.04	0.10
	Understory	10	0.04	0.01	0.03	0.08
	All	28	0.05	0.01	0.05	0.20
Henriettea macfadyenii (Triana) Alain	Overstory	2	0.53	0.01	0.01	0.54
	All	2	0.53	0.01	0.01	0.54
H. squamulosum (Cogn.) W.S. Judd	Overstory	2	0.30	0.02	0.03	0.32
	Understory	2	0.06	0.06	0.08	0.12
	All	4	0.18	0.07	0.15	0.32
Hernandia sonora L.	Understory	1	0.02			0.02
	All	1	0.02			0.02
Hibiscus elatus Sw.	Understory	1	0.06			0.06
	All	1	0.06			0.06
Hirtella rugosa Thuill. ex Pers.	Understory	2	0.04	0.04	0.06	0.08
	All	2	0.04	0.04	0.06	0.08
Homalium racemosum Jacq.	Overstory	7	0.21	0.08	0.21	0.68
	Understory	2	0.08	0.06	0.08	0.14
	All	10	0.21	0.07	0.21	0.68
Hymenaea courbaril L.	Overstory	13	0.33	0.04	0.15	0.62
	Understory	9	0.20	0.07	0.21	0.60
	All	26	0.36	0.05	0.24	0.91
Ilex nitida (Vahl) Maxim.	Understory	1	0.00			0.00
	All	1	0.00			0.00
Inga laurina (Sw.) Willd.	Overstory	29	0.69	0.15	0.82	3.32
	Understory	10	0.32	0.14	0.43	1.44
	All	70	0.50	0.07	0.60	3.32

continued

Table A.2—Diameter at breast height (1.4 m) periodic annual increments (PAI, cm) by species and crown position, with number of trees measured, standard error of the mean, standard deviation of the mean, and maximum observed PAI increase from Puerto Rico forest inventory data (continued)

Species[a]	Crown position[b]	N	Periodic annual increments			
			Mean	SE	SD	Max
Inga nobilis Willd. ssp. *quaternata* (Poepp. & Endl.) T.D. Penn.	Overstory	1	0.13			0.13
	Understory	1	0.54			0.54
	All	2	0.34	0.21	0.29	0.54
I. vera Willd.	Overstory	70	0.42	0.06	0.53	2.54
	Understory	16	0.35	0.08	0.31	1.26
	All	129	0.46	0.05	0.56	2.88
Ixora ferrea (Jacq.) Benth.	Overstory	2	0.89	0.25	0.35	1.14
	All	2	0.89	0.25	0.35	1.14
Krugiodendron ferreum (Vahl) Urb.	Overstory	4	0.11	0.06	0.12	0.28
	Understory	6	0.03	0.01	0.02	0.06
	All	10	0.06	0.03	0.08	0.28
Laguncularia racemosa (L.) C.F. Gaertn.	Overstory	1	0.00			0.00
	Understory	6	0.15	0.02	0.06	0.24
	All	7	0.13	0.03	0.08	0.24
Leucaena leucocephala (Lam.) de Wit	Overstory	51	0.24	0.03	0.19	0.84
	Understory	13	0.10	0.02	0.07	0.20
	All	64	0.21	0.02	0.18	0.84
Licaria brittoniana Allen & Gregory	Understory	1	0.18			0.18
	All	1	0.18			0.18
L. parvifolia (Lam.) Kosterm.	Overstory	1	0.48			0.48
	Understory	2	0.01	0.01	0.01	0.02
	All	4	0.18	0.11	0.22	0.48
Lonchocarpus glaucifolius Urb.	Overstory	1	0.06			0.06
	Understory	1	0.10			0.10
	All	2	0.08	0.02	0.03	0.10
L. heptaphyllus (Poir.) DC.	Overstory	3	0.24	0.07	0.12	0.36
	All	3	0.24	0.07	0.12	0.36
Magnolia portoricensis Bello	Overstory	2	0.53	0.38	0.53	0.90
	All	3	0.35	0.28	0.48	0.90
Mammea americana L.	Overstory	2	0.71	0.40	0.57	1.11
	Understory	1	0.02			0.02
	All	3	0.48	0.33	0.56	1.11
Mangifera indica L.	Overstory	31	0.38	0.09	0.48	2.28
	Understory	8	0.26	0.11	0.32	0.94
	All	68	0.40	0.05	0.39	2.28
Manilkara bidentata (A. DC.) A. Chev	Overstory	2	0.83	0.22	0.31	1.05
	All	2	0.83	0.22	0.31	1.05
Margaritaria nobilis L. f.	Overstory	1	0.02			0.02
	Understory	2	0.04	0.04	0.06	0.08
	All	3	0.03	0.02	0.04	0.08

continued

Table A.2—Diameter at breast height (1.4 m) periodic annual increments (PAI, cm) by species and crown position, with number of trees measured, standard error of the mean, standard deviation of the mean, and maximum observed PAI increase from Puerto Rico forest inventory data (continued)

Species[a]	Crown position[b]	N	Periodic annual increments			
			Mean	SE	SD	Max
Matayba domingensis (DC.) Radlk.	Overstory	3	0.12	0.02	0.04	0.16
	All	4	0.24	0.08	0.17	0.47
Maytenus ponceana Britton	Understory	2	0.08	0.08	0.11	0.16
	All	2	0.08	0.08	0.11	0.16
Melicoccus bijugatus Jacq.	Overstory	8	0.63	0.13	0.37	1.16
	Understory	5	0.26	0.10	0.23	0.58
	All	13	0.49	0.10	0.37	1.16
Meliosma herbertii Rolfe	Overstory	6	0.13	0.03	0.08	0.22
	Understory	1	0.14			0.14
	All	8	0.14	0.02	0.07	0.22
Miconia impetiolaris (Sw.) D. Don ex DC.	Overstory	1	0.49			0.49
	Understory	1	0.08			0.08
	All	2	0.29	0.21	0.29	0.49
M. laevigata (L.) D. Don	Overstory	5	0.39	0.08	0.18	0.68
	Understory	2	0.34	0.14	0.20	0.48
	All	7	0.38	0.06	0.17	0.68
M. prasina (Sw.) DC.	Overstory	3	0.52	0.12	0.22	0.74
	Understory	6	0.15	0.09	0.21	0.52
	All	16	0.22	0.06	0.26	0.74
M. pycnoneura Urb.	Understory	1	0.12			0.12
	All	1	0.12			0.12
M. subcorymbosa Britton	Overstory	1	0.33			0.33
	All	1	0.33			0.33
M. tetrandra (Sw.) D. Don	Overstory	2	0.11	0.01	0.01	0.12
	Understory	3	0.51	0.10	0.17	0.68
	All	5	0.35	0.11	0.25	0.68
Micropholis garciniifolia Pierre	Overstory	13	0.12	0.05	0.20	0.72
	All	17	0.28	0.08	0.35	0.96
M. guyanensis (A. DC.) Pierre	Overstory	21	0.18	0.03	0.13	0.46
	Understory	4	0.13	0.06	0.11	0.28
	All	33	0.16	0.02	0.12	0.46
Myrcia citrifolia (Aubl.) Urb.	Overstory	1	0.10			0.10
	All	1	0.10			0.10
M. deflexa (Poir.) DC.	Overstory	1	0.31			0.31
	Understory	3	0.15	0.05	0.09	0.24
	All	7	0.16	0.05	0.12	0.31
M. fallax (Rich.) DC.	Understory	2	0.03	0.01	0.01	0.04
	All	2	0.03	0.01	0.01	0.04

continued

Table A.2—Diameter at breast height (1.4 m) periodic annual increments (PAI, cm) by species and crown position, with number of trees measured, standard error of the mean, standard deviation of the mean, and maximum observed PAI increase from Puerto Rico forest inventory data (continued)

Species[a]	Crown position[b]	N	Periodic annual increments			
			Mean	SE	SD	Max
Myrcia splendens (Sw.) DC.	Overstory	3	0.28	0.14	0.24	0.54
	Understory	13	0.21	0.07	0.24	0.62
	All	29	0.20	0.04	0.19	0.62
Myrsine coriacea (Sw.) R. Br. ex Roem. & J.A. Schult.	Overstory	4	0.47	0.04	0.09	0.54
	Understory	2	0.24	0.08	0.11	0.32
	All	7	0.36	0.06	0.16	0.54
M. cubana A. DC.	Overstory	3	0.43	0.07	0.12	0.52
	Understory	1	0.02			0.02
	All	5	0.33	0.09	0.20	0.52
Nectandra coriacea (Sw.) Griseb.	Overstory	4	0.15	0.03	0.05	0.22
	Understory	4	0.22	0.09	0.18	0.40
	All	9	0.20	0.05	0.14	0.40
N. hihua (Ruiz & Pav.) Rohwer	Overstory	1	1.50			1.50
	All	1	1.50			1.50
N. turbacensis (Kunth) Nees	Overstory	3	0.73	0.00	0.00	0.73
	Understory	2	0.08	0.02	0.03	0.10
	All	6	0.53	0.14	0.35	0.82
Neea buxifolia (Hook. f.) Heimerl	Understory	1	0.02			0.02
	All	1	0.02			0.02
Neolaugeria resinosa (Vahl) Nicolson	Overstory	13	0.30	0.07	0.26	0.70
	Understory	10	0.21	0.06	0.20	0.74
	All	30	0.28	0.04	0.23	0.74
Ocotea floribunda (Sw.) Mez	Overstory	2	0.31	0.03	0.04	0.34
	All	2	0.31	0.03	0.04	0.34
O. leucoxylon (Sw.) De Laness.	Overstory	18	0.27	0.05	0.20	0.66
	Understory	22	0.21	0.06	0.27	0.78
	All	61	0.27	0.04	0.30	1.69
O. moschata (Pav. ex Meisn.) Mez	Overstory	2	0.35	0.17	0.24	0.52
	All	2	0.35	0.17	0.24	0.52
O. wrightii (Meisn.) Mez	Overstory	1	0.58			0.58
	All	1	0.58			0.58
Ormosia krugii Urb.	Overstory	11	0.23	0.06	0.20	0.66
	Understory	4	0.05	0.03	0.05	0.12
	All	18	0.21	0.04	0.16	0.66
Ouratea littoralis Urb.	Understory	1	0.08			0.08
	All	1	0.08			0.08
Palicourea croceoides Ham.	Overstory	3	0.07	0.02	0.04	0.11
	Understory	2	0.11	0.03	0.04	0.13
	All	5	0.08	0.02	0.04	0.13

continued

Table A.2—Diameter at breast height (1.4 m) periodic annual increments (PAI, cm) by species and crown position, with number of trees measured, standard error of the mean, standard deviation of the mean, and maximum observed PAI increase from Puerto Rico forest inventory data (continued)

Species[a]	Crown position[b]	N	Periodic annual increments			
			Mean	SE	SD	Max
Parathesis crenulata (Vent.) Hook. f.	Overstory	1	0.58			0.58
	All	1	0.58			0.58
Peltophorum pterocarpum (DC.) Backer ex K. Heyne	Overstory	5	0.64	0.04	0.09	0.72
	All	5	0.64	0.04	0.09	0.72
Persea americana Mill.	Overstory	6	0.63	0.25	0.62	1.80
	Understory	3	1.26	0.52	0.90	2.28
	All	11	0.70	0.22	0.73	2.28
Petitia domingensis Jacq.	Overstory	3	0.20	0.04	0.08	0.28
	Understory	2	0.04	0.02	0.03	0.06
	All	7	0.19	0.05	0.13	0.37
Picramnia pentandra Sw.	Understory	1	0.08			0.08
	All	1	0.08			0.08
Pictetia aculeata (Vahl) Urb.	Overstory	13	0.06	0.02	0.06	0.16
	Understory	3	0.09	0.05	0.08	0.16
	All	16	0.06	0.02	0.06	0.16
Pilosocereus royenii (L.) Byles & Rowley	Overstory	2	0.32	0.30	0.42	0.62
	All	2	0.32	0.30	0.42	0.62
Pimenta racemosa (Mill.) J.W. Moore	Overstory	7	0.28	0.08	0.22	0.66
	All	7	0.28	0.08	0.22	0.66
Piper aduncum L.	Understory	1	0.15			0.15
	All	1	0.15			0.15
Pisonia albida (Heimerl) Britton ex Standl.	Overstory	2	0.05	0.01	0.01	0.06
	Understory	3	0.25	0.16	0.27	0.56
	All	5	0.17	0.10	0.22	0.56
P. subcordata Sw.	Understory	1	0.14			0.14
	All	1	0.14			0.14
Pithecellobium dulce (Roxb.) Benth.	Overstory	5	1.64	0.38	0.84	2.74
	All	5	1.64	0.38	0.84	2.74
P. unguis-cati (L.) Benth.	Overstory	5	1.18	1.14	2.55	5.74
	All	5	1.18	1.14	2.55	5.74
Plumeria obtusa L.	Overstory	3	0.21	0.02	0.04	0.24
	All	3	0.21	0.02	0.04	0.24
Podocarpus coriaceus Rich.	Overstory	1	0.05			0.05
	All	1	0.05			0.05
Poitea florida (Vahl) Lavin	Overstory	1	0.04			0.04
	All	1	0.04			0.04
Pouteria multiflora (A. DC.) Eyma	Overstory	7	0.55	0.41	1.09	3.00
	Understory	2	0.54	0.00	0.00	0.54
	All	9	0.55	0.31	0.94	3.00

continued

Table A.2—Diameter at breast height (1.4 m) periodic annual increments (PAI, cm) by species and crown position, with number of trees measured, standard error of the mean, standard deviation of the mean, and maximum observed PAI increase from Puerto Rico forest inventory data (continued)

Species[a]	Crown position[b]	N	Periodic annual increments			
			Mean	SE	SD	Max
Pouteria sapota (Jacq.) H.E. Moore & Stearn	Overstory	2	0.35	0.11	0.16	0.46
	All	2	0.35	0.11	0.16	0.46
Prestoea acuminata (Willd.) H.E. Moore var. *montana* (Graham) A. Hend. & G. Galeano	Overstory	41	0.04	0.01	0.06	0.20
	Understory	47	0.17	0.03	0.21	1.00
	All	110	0.10	0.02	0.16	1.00
Prosopis pallida (Humb. & Bonpl. ex Willd.) Kunth	Overstory	3	0.11	0.11	0.18	0.32
	All	3	0.11	0.11	0.18	0.32
Prunus myrtifolia (L.) Urb.	Understory	1	0.09			0.09
	All	1	0.09			0.09
Pseudolmedia spuria (Sw.) Griseb.	Overstory	1	0.18			0.18
	All	1	0.18			0.18
Psidium amplexicaule Pers.	Understory	5	0.07	0.03	0.06	0.16
	All	5	0.07	0.03	0.06	0.16
P. guajava L.	Overstory	6	0.07	0.05	0.12	0.31
	Understory	5	0.02	0.01	0.03	0.06
	All	14	0.05	0.02	0.09	0.31
Psychotria berteriana DC.	Understory	1	0.04			0.04
	All	1	0.04			0.04
Psychotria brachiata Sw.	Understory	2	0.01	0.01	0.01	0.02
	All	2	0.01	0.01	0.01	0.02
Quararibea turbinata (Sw.) Poir.	Understory	7	0.15	0.05	0.13	0.40
	All	8	0.15	0.04	0.12	0.40
Randia aculeata L.	Overstory	3	0.17	0.04	0.08	0.26
	Understory	2	0.16	0.08	0.11	0.24
	All	5	0.17	0.03	0.08	0.26
Rhizophora mangle L.	Overstory	2	0.00	0.00	0.00	0.00
	Understory	1	0.00			0.00
	All	3	0.00	0.00	0.00	0.00
Roystonea borinquena O.F. Cook	Overstory	16	0.26	0.11	0.45	1.28
	Understory	3	2.41	1.05	1.81	4.00
	All	27	0.46	0.18	0.94	4.00
Sagraea umbrosa (Sw.) DC.	Overstory	5	0.20	0.03	0.08	0.28
	Understory	1	0.45			0.45
	All	6	0.24	0.05	0.12	0.45
Samanea saman (Jacq.) Merr.	Overstory	1	2.30			2.30
	All	1	2.30			2.30
Sapindus saponaria L.	Overstory	1	0.25			0.25
	All	1	0.75			0.75

continued

Table A.2—Diameter at breast height (1.4 m) periodic annual increments (PAI, cm) by species and crown position, with number of trees measured, standard error of the mean, standard deviation of the mean, and maximum observed PAI increase from Puerto Rico forest inventory data (continued)

Species[a]	Crown position[b]	N	Periodic annual increments			
			Mean	SE	SD	Max
Sapium laurocerasus Desf.	Overstory	1	0.34			0.34
	Understory	1	0.88			0.88
	All	3	0.50	0.19	0.33	0.88
Savia sessiliflora (Sw.) Willd.	Understory	2	0.06	0.04	0.06	0.10
	All	2	0.06	0.04	0.06	0.10
Schefflera morototoni (Aubl.) Maguire, Steyerm. & Frodin	Overstory	23	0.33	0.05	0.25	0.88
	Understory	7	0.55	0.22	0.59	1.70
	All	53	0.42	0.04	0.32	1.70
Schoepfia obovata C. Wright	Overstory	1	0.00			0.00
	All	1	0.00			0.00
Senna siamea (Lam.) Irwin & Barneby	Overstory	7	0.66	0.27	0.70	2.02
	Understory	2	0.98	0.50	0.71	1.48
	All	9	0.64	0.20	0.61	2.02
Sideroxylon cubense (Griseb.) T.D. Penn.	Overstory	1	0.02			0.02
	Understory	1	0.11			0.11
	All	3	0.15	0.09	0.16	0.33
S. salicifolium (L.) Lam.	Overstory	7	0.20	0.05	0.14	0.41
	Understory	2	0.08	0.04	0.06	0.12
	All	11	0.22	0.05	0.16	0.57
Sloanea berteriana Choisy ex DC.	Overstory	4	0.13	0.02	0.05	0.20
	Understory	5	0.05	0.02	0.04	0.10
	All	13	0.17	0.05	0.16	0.56
Solanum rugosum Dunal	Understory	2	0.09	0.09	0.13	0.18
	All	2	0.09	0.09	0.13	0.18
Spathodea campanulata P. Beauv.	Overstory	183	0.82	0.05	0.67	3.76
	Understory	148	0.33	0.03	0.39	2.14
	All	371	0.64	0.03	0.63	3.76
Spondias dulcis Parkinson	Overstory	2	0.24	0.24	0.33	0.47
	All	2	0.24	0.24	0.33	0.47
S. mombin L.	Overstory	13	0.61	0.10	0.36	1.18
	Understory	3	0.35	0.07	0.12	0.43
	All	21	0.48	0.08	0.37	1.18
Swietenia macrophylla King	Overstory	3	0.33	0.20	0.34	0.72
	All	3	0.33	0.20	0.34	0.72
S. mahagoni (L.) Jacq.	Overstory	10	0.19	0.05	0.16	0.48
	Understory	1	0.16			0.16
	All	11	0.19	0.05	0.15	0.48
Symplocos martinicensis Jacq.	Overstory	4	0.39	0.11	0.22	0.64
	All	4	0.36	0.12	0.24	0.64

continued

Table A.2—Diameter at breast height (1.4 m) periodic annual increments (PAI, cm) by species and crown position, with number of trees measured, standard error of the mean, standard deviation of the mean, and maximum observed PAI increase from Puerto Rico forest inventory data (continued)

Species[a]	Crown position[b]	N	Periodic annual increments			
			Mean	SE	SD	Max
Syzygium jambos (L.) Alston	Overstory	27	0.12	0.03	0.14	0.54
	Understory	56	0.13	0.03	0.19	0.90
	All	120	0.14	0.02	0.20	0.90
Tabebuia heterophylla (DC.) Britton	Overstory	77	0.34	0.04	0.35	1.46
	Understory	27	0.18	0.04	0.21	0.78
	All	142	0.29	0.03	0.30	1.46
T. rigida Urb.	Overstory	1	0.00			0.00
	All	1	0.00			0.00
Tamarindus indica L.	Overstory	1	1.08			1.08
	All	2	1.30	0.22	0.31	1.52
Terminalia catappa L.	Overstory	6	0.54	0.12	0.30	0.83
	Understory	1	0.42			0.42
	All	8	0.53	0.09	0.25	0.83
Tetragastris balsamifera (Sw.) Oken	Overstory	4	0.31	0.14	0.28	0.60
	Understory	3	0.46	0.17	0.29	0.80
	All	7	0.37	0.10	0.27	0.80
Tetrazygia elaeagnoides (Sw.) DC.	Overstory	11	0.21	0.08	0.27	0.96
	Understory	5	0.18	0.04	0.10	0.34
	All	22	0.16	0.04	0.20	0.96
Thespesia grandiflora DC.	Overstory	6	0.38	0.16	0.39	1.14
	Understory	3	0.11	0.05	0.08	0.20
	All	14	0.24	0.07	0.28	1.14
Thouinia striata Radlk.	Overstory	10	0.17	0.08	0.26	0.84
	Understory	5	0.19	0.09	0.19	0.50
	All	17	0.20	0.05	0.23	0.84
T. striata Radlk. var. *portoricensis* (Radlk.) Votava & Alain	Overstory	7	0.03	0.01	0.04	0.10
	Understory	5	0.02	0.02	0.03	0.08
	All	12	0.03	0.01	0.04	0.10
Trema micrantha (L.) Blume	Overstory	1	0.54			0.54
	Understory	1	0.06			0.06
	All	2	0.30	0.24	0.34	0.54
Trichilia hirta L.	Overstory	2	0.50	0.24	0.34	0.74
	Understory	1	0.00			0.00
	All	3	0.33	0.22	0.38	0.74
T. pallida Sw.	Understory	11	0.10	0.04	0.13	0.44
	All	21	0.10	0.03	0.12	0.44
Turpinia occidentalis (Sw.) G. Don	Overstory	10	0.26	0.09	0.27	0.78
	Understory	1	0.01			0.01
	All	11	0.27	0.09	0.29	0.78

continued

Table A.2—Diameter at breast height (1.4 m) periodic annual increments (PAI, cm) by species and crown position, with number of trees measured, standard error of the mean, standard deviation of the mean, and maximum observed PAI increase from Puerto Rico forest inventory data (continued)

Species[a]	Crown position[b]	N	Periodic annual increments			
			Mean	SE	SD	Max
Urera baccifera (L.) Gaudich.	Understory	1	0.04			0.04
	All	1	0.04			0.04
Vitex divaricata Sw.	Overstory	4	0.31	0.17	0.34	0.76
	Understory	1	0.12			0.12
	All	6	0.23	0.12	0.29	0.76
Xylosma buxifolia A. Gray	Understory	1	0.05			0.05
	All	1	0.05			0.05
X. pachyphylla (Krug & Urb.) Urb.	Overstory	1	0.14			0.14
	All	1	0.14			0.14
Zanthoxylum martinicense (Lam.) DC.	Overstory	23	0.57	0.12	0.57	2.62
	Understory	8	0.25	0.07	0.18	0.48
	All	40	0.40	0.08	0.49	2.62
Z. monophyllum (Lam.) P. Wilson	Overstory	2	0.36	0.12	0.17	0.48
	Understory	2	0.03	0.01	0.01	0.04
	All	4	0.20	0.11	0.21	0.48

— = insufficient sample; N = number of trees measured; SE = standard error of the mean; SD = standard deviation of the mean; Max = maximum observed.

[a] USDA Natural Resources Conservation Service (2006).

[b] Trees in the overstory crown positon have crowns that are exposed to direct sunlight from above and some light from the side, while understory trees receive little or no direct sunlight.

Table A.3—Diameter at breast height (1.4 m) periodic annual increments (PAI, cm) for commercial species by tree class with number of trees measured, standard error of the mean, standard deviation of the mean, and maximum observed PAI increase from Puerto Rico forest inventory data

Species[a]	Tree class[b]	N	Periodic annual increments			
			Mean	SE	SD	Max
Albizia procera (Roxb.) Benth.	Growing stock	10	0.99	0.24	0.75	2.22
	Cull	20	0.48	0.11	0.48	2.16
Andira inermis (W. Wright) Kunth ex DC.	Growing stock	54	0.32	0.04	0.31	1.26
	Cull	115	0.19	0.02	0.20	1.05
Avicennia germinans (L.) L.	Growing stock	2	0.60	0.60	0.85	1.20
	Cull	13	0.16	0.08	0.30	1.12
Buchenavia tetraphylla (Aubl.) Howard	Growing stock	5	0.37	0.10	0.23	0.63
	Cull	2	1.23	0.23	0.32	1.45
Bursera simaruba (L.) Sarg.	Growing stock	9	0.54	0.26	0.78	2.48
	Cull	58	0.30	0.04	0.30	1.44
Byrsonima spicata (Cav.) Kunth	Growing stock	7	0.46	0.13	0.34	1.01
	Cull	12	0.42	0.13	0.44	1.56
Calophyllum antillanum Britton	Growing stock	27	0.42	0.06	0.33	1.38
	Cull	14	0.41	0.08	0.32	0.88
Cecropia schreberiana Miq.	Growing stock	86	0.73	0.07	0.65	2.96
	Cull	51	0.93	0.13	0.94	4.30
Cedrela odorata L.	Growing stock	7	0.22	0.06	0.17	0.54
	Cull	4	0.12	0.10	0.20	0.41
Conocarpus erectus L.	Cull	4	0.25	0.23	0.46	0.94
Cordia alliodora (Ruiz & Pav.) Oken	Growing stock	17	0.34	0.08	0.32	1.16
	Cull	9	0.28	0.09	0.26	0.72
Cupania americana L.	Growing stock	5	0.43	0.15	0.33	0.83
	Cull	16	0.50	0.08	0.31	1.00
Dacryodes excelsa Vahl	Growing stock	14	0.44	0.08	0.28	1.08
	Cull	5	0.50	0.14	0.32	0.90
Eucalyptus robusta Sm.	Growing stock	16	0.28	0.08	0.33	0.96
	Cull	13	0.87	0.45	1.62	5.84
Ficus citrifolia Mill.	Growing stock	3	0.54	0.51	0.88	1.55
	Cull	13	0.58	0.24	0.85	3.05
Guapira fragrans (Dum. Cours.) Little	Growing stock	6	0.20	0.06	0.15	0.44
	Cull	38	0.29	0.06	0.36	1.50
Guarea guidonia (L.) Sleumer	Growing stock	104	0.69	0.05	0.55	2.90
	Cull	248	0.48	0.03	0.51	2.85
Guazuma ulmifolia Lam.	Growing stock	2	0.38	0.26	0.36	0.63
	Cull	19	0.54	0.10	0.43	1.80
Gymnanthes lucida Sw.	Growing stock	3	0.13	0.04	0.07	0.20
	Cull	25	0.04	0.01	0.03	0.10

continued

Table A.3—Diameter at breast height (1.4 m) periodic annual increments (PAI, cm) for commercial species by tree class with number of trees measured, standard error of the mean, standard deviation of the mean, and maximum observed PAI increase from Puerto Rico forest inventory data (continued)

Species[a]	Tree class[b]	N	Periodic annual increments			
			Mean	SE	SD	Max
Hibiscus elatus Sw.	Cull	1	0.06			0.06
Homalium racemosum Jacq.	Growing stock	1	0.68			0.68
	Cull	9	0.16	0.04	0.13	0.49
Hymenaea courbaril L.	Growing stock	8	0.41	0.11	0.32	0.91
	Cull	18	0.33	0.05	0.20	0.75
Inga laurina (Sw.) Willd.	Growing stock	31	0.63	0.13	0.74	3.32
	Cull	39	0.40	0.07	0.44	2.22
Inga vera Willd.	Growing stock	54	0.42	0.06	0.43	1.90
	Cull	75	0.49	0.07	0.65	2.88
Laguncularia racemosa (L.) C.F. Gaertn.	Cull	7	0.13	0.03	0.08	0.24
Mangifera indica L.	Growing stock	9	0.37	0.07	0.22	0.89
	Cull	59	0.40	0.05	0.41	2.28
Manilkara bidentata (A. DC.) A. Chev	Growing stock	2	0.83	0.22	0.31	1.05
Neolaugeria resinosa (Vahl) Nicolson	Growing stock	12	0.46	0.07	0.23	0.74
	Cull	18	0.16	0.03	0.13	0.60
Ocotea floribunda (Sw.) Mez	Cull	2	0.31	0.03	0.04	0.34
O. leucoxylon (Sw.) De Laness.	Growing stock	20	0.27	0.05	0.23	0.78
	Cull	41	0.27	0.05	0.33	1.69
Ormosia krugii Urb.	Growing stock	11	0.24	0.05	0.17	0.66
	Cull	7	0.16	0.05	0.14	0.38
Petitia domingensis Jacq.	Growing stock	3	0.20	0.10	0.18	0.37
	Cull	4	0.18	0.05	0.11	0.30
Pimenta racemosa (Mill.) J.W. Moore	Cull	7	0.28	0.08	0.22	0.66
Pouteria multiflora (A. DC.) Eyma	Growing stock	7	0.69	0.39	1.04	3.00
	Cull	2	0.05	0.05	0.07	0.10
Senna siamea (Lam.) Irwin & Barneby	Growing stock	3	0.68	0.24	0.41	1.12
	Cull	6	0.61	0.30	0.73	2.02
Spondias mombin L.	Growing stock	6	0.19	0.08	0.20	0.47
	Cull	15	0.59	0.09	0.36	1.18
Swietenia macrophylla King	Cull	3	0.33	0.20	0.34	0.72
S. mahagoni (L.) Jacq.	Growing stock	3	0.27	0.03	0.05	0.30
	Cull	8	0.16	0.06	0.17	0.48
Terminalia catappa L.	Growing stock	6	0.53	0.12	0.29	0.83
	Cull	2	0.51	0.08	0.12	0.59

continued

Table A.3—Diameter at breast height (1.4 m) periodic annual increments (PAI, cm) for commercial species by tree class with number of trees measured, standard error of the mean, standard deviation of the mean, and maximum observed PAI increase from Puerto Rico forest inventory data (continued)

| Species[a] | Tree class[b] | N | Periodic annual increments | | | |
			Mean	SE	SD	Max
Thespesia grandiflora DC.	Growing stock	3	0.11	0.01	0.03	0.13
	Cull	11	0.28	0.09	0.31	1.14
Vitex divaricata Sw.	Growing stock	3	0.13	0.12	0.20	0.36
	Cull	3	0.33	0.22	0.38	0.76
Zanthoxylum martinicense (Lam.) DC.	Growing stock	11	0.34	0.11	0.37	1.04
	Cull	29	0.41	0.10	0.53	2.62
All commercial species combined	Growing stock	570	0.51	0.02	0.52	3.32
	Cull	1,045	0.40	0.02	0.52	5.84

— = insufficient sample; N = number of trees measured; SE = standard error of the mean; SD = standard deviation of the mean; Max = maximum observed.

[a] USDA Natural Resources Conservation Service (2006).

[b] To meet requirements for the growing-stock tree class, trees must have one-third or more of the gross board-foot volume in the entire saw-log section with commercial logs meeting grade, soundness, and size requirements or the potential to do so for poletimber-sized trees. A growing-stock tree must have one 3.5-m or two 2.5-m logs, now or prospectively, for live poletimber-sized trees to qualify as growing stock. Trees that do not meet these requirements are considered cull.

www.ingramcontent.com/pod-product-compliance
Lightning Source LLC
Chambersburg PA
CBHW081130280526
45787CB00007B/3036